Moments of
POETRY

BY THRE3DEE BOOK 1 VERSION 2

Moments of POETRY

Copyright 2020 © Thre3Dee

All rights reserved. No part of this publication may be reproduced or distributed in any form or by any means, electronic or mechanical, including photocopying, recording, or by any information storage or retrieval system, without the prior written consent of the author.

ISBN: 978-1-62676-574-0

Moments of POETRY

Love You So Much

I love you so much
That I feel right.
If I don't get to speak to you,
I have difficulty sleeping at night,
I've never been in love before
Never felt so good and bright.
If your love for me is true
I want to hold you in my arms till the end of the night
So I can tell you how I feel for you. Alright!
Please, don't think this is a lie
Because it was hard to try.
How do I get my heart to stop crying?
My feelings to stop trying
When you wouldn't
Feel for me even if I was dying…

Moments of POETRY

Day & Night

Not every day is bright,

It is not in every night we get light

But as long as I'm around

Do as you please because

I won't let you out my sight.

As long as we are together:

If we appreciate each other

And be polite,

We won't have to worry of

Letting go

On one dark night.

Moments of POETRY

Love & Attention

Love is a relation
More than a situation.
This needs 100% attention
And affection,
So that we can live this life to perfection.
Girl, offering you my protection
Ignoring the world's corruption
Along with the World wars and scores.
Everyone knows that
'life is a journey,
and I'm ready to walk you through it'
So, don't ever worry baby
Because I'm around.
If you're in difficulties; I'll rush to your town
To make sure you are healthy
Love purely and surely —
Don't ever cheat.
Eventually, the results will be neat.
Come into my arms
I want to

Moments of POETRY

Compatible

I would love to stand,
Next to your side.
So that I can encourage you
And be your only pride.
I would like to look at you
From above,
So that I can send down to you all my love.
If I were a star in the sky,
You'll always be able to see me.
Say Hi!!!
If like all the stars, I was to shine
You would be able to see
How much I need you
And want you to be mine.

Moments of POETRY

Must Love!

Love is a need, love is a must.
You only fall in love
So that people can break your trust.
When your trust is broken
You are worn and torn, left to feel upset,
To think why you were born.
But, be honest and think about someone
Who lies and when you are upset,
Never tries to wipe your tears
And get rid of your fears.
How can they be trusted?
Because, the moment they lay their eyes
Elsewhere your love can get busted....

Moments of POETRY

Need!

I love you so much that you
Have become my need.
I need you in my life so that I can succeed.
Why waste time and commit a crime,
When all I did was love; so that you could be mine.
Why is it that whenever and whatever you want you never get?
Years later when you see people
You look in their eyes yet do nothing but regret.
Love is so lovely
That even love hurts.
So many players and so many games
But still, I think about love.
My thoughts hurt; love is not a game
It's just a lifetime pain to remain.

Moments of POETRY

Lonely, Lonely

I've been lonely for years
Although single for months.
I never gave myself a thought, not even once.
Just once, I looked into your eyes
And realized
It's time to be hypnotized.
Kissing your dimple
And making love to you,
Because you are simply special,
Your love is like a potion
From the sweetest of oceans
Which I want you to spread
All over my body like a lotion.
Hope you understand my plan
Along with my dreams.
I love you girl
So, let me get closer
Then those skin tight jeans.
If love is a book, I'm a writer.
If it's an art, I'm a brush, strokes brighter.
Give me one chance to romance.
Every time you think of me,
You'll get the urge to dance.
One chance is all it takes
Now you don't want to be crying.
By saying no
And making a mistake.
Because, in reality
We are not always
Fortunate to get a
Retake...

Moments of POETRY

Night!

Where I look, you are all I sight.
No matter where I am,
You're the only name I recite.
I love you and don't want to fight.
I want to spend together every morning,
After every lovely night.
I want to touch you and tease you,
Do everything it takes to please you.
I want to hold you in my arms and squeeze you,
Don't ever walk away
As it's not a toy; it's my heart.
I need you baby
As without you, I'm falling apart.
You're that one miracle
That blessed my life since the start.
I noticed you, and hold you as an art.
Your picture is kept safe in my heart.
Wanting you day and night
Has forever made me feel so right!
I want you back in my arms
Before the end
Of the night.

Moments of POETRY

Love Games

Love is a game
In which some players are insane
With a small brain.
Ladies like you are filled
With real emotions and tears.
You are crying for them fake guys.
You fell for his crap
And all his lies.
You even gave other fools a try
For crying out loud,
I love you baby.
Give me a try,
You can walk past
All the fools waving goodbye.
When you walk together into our new life,
Don't forget to say "Hi",
We need to stay together —
Hand in hand
Give it a try.
If we ever go wrong;
Don't want to ask why?
We're going to live with honesty,
Not any lie.
If you don't like this, then it's time
To say good bye

Moments of POETRY

Minutes!!

Minutes together and moments away
We should sit for a moment and pray
That however long life is to last
Together we will stay.
Love to love, hate to hate.
No matter what, don't hesitate
We both share feelings
Good or bad.
You don't want to lose your loved one,
Living sad
Running to you hear, I am.
I Love you
I'll do whatever I can.
We should be chilling and willing
The life we share
Can be blessed for our living
So, don't leave me
For a moment we share,
Because, no one will love you
Like me.
When it comes to you,
I truly care.

Moments of POETRY

Baby Cakes

Baby cakes, I got to confess
I make loads of mistakes
So, my life was a mess,
really full of stress.
No matter what I do, there is no success
You are mine and what I have achieved.
You are all I need
I know you are the one who is only mine.
Have faith and I'll change every style of mine
All I need for eternity is you to smile.
Laugh and never cry,
Because it will only make it hard for me to try.
No matter what, I will be by your side
You got me, so don't fear.
I'll always be there to wipe every tear.
Sitting, we are far away
Wishing, I was like your heartbeat
All the way I love you and that's all I want to say
I'm here for real and not to play...

Moments of POETRY

Darkness

Darkness-falls is a fact!
In your life it can have a deep impact.
Why tell someone your worst fear
When all they do is shed
An artificial tear?
Come close and join your fears
Leaving your heart
To cry those tears
Is it love or just a lie?
Why do I have to be left to cry?
All I did was love not war.
I want you back in my life
So, please say no more.
You know who and where I am;
If you want to meet me
Tell me.
I'll be there as soon as I can.
Convince your family, and your mum
One day, when you be my bride
I'll sing you a love song.

Moments of POETRY

Life!

My life is so lonely, it includes
Me and me alone.
I face so many difficulties in finding a wife
That would love me and me only.
If we get married
I will never let you feel lonely.
I won't ever let us be apart
I will only love you
From my heart .
Don't waste any more time
From being mine.
Without you, my heart
Feels agony and pain.
Don't commit this crime.
We will never be the same

Moments of POETRY

Fight & War

Why do people war and fight
When will they stop and see the light?
Why don't people stop arguing?
And stop the ongoing fight?
When we all know it's not right.
Think of your future before your past.
You don't want to get hit in the future,
with the imagery of 'blast'
from the past.
There's no saying, how long it will last.
Why not be wise and realize
that honesty pays and don't tell lies.
Don't fight time to be bright and unite…

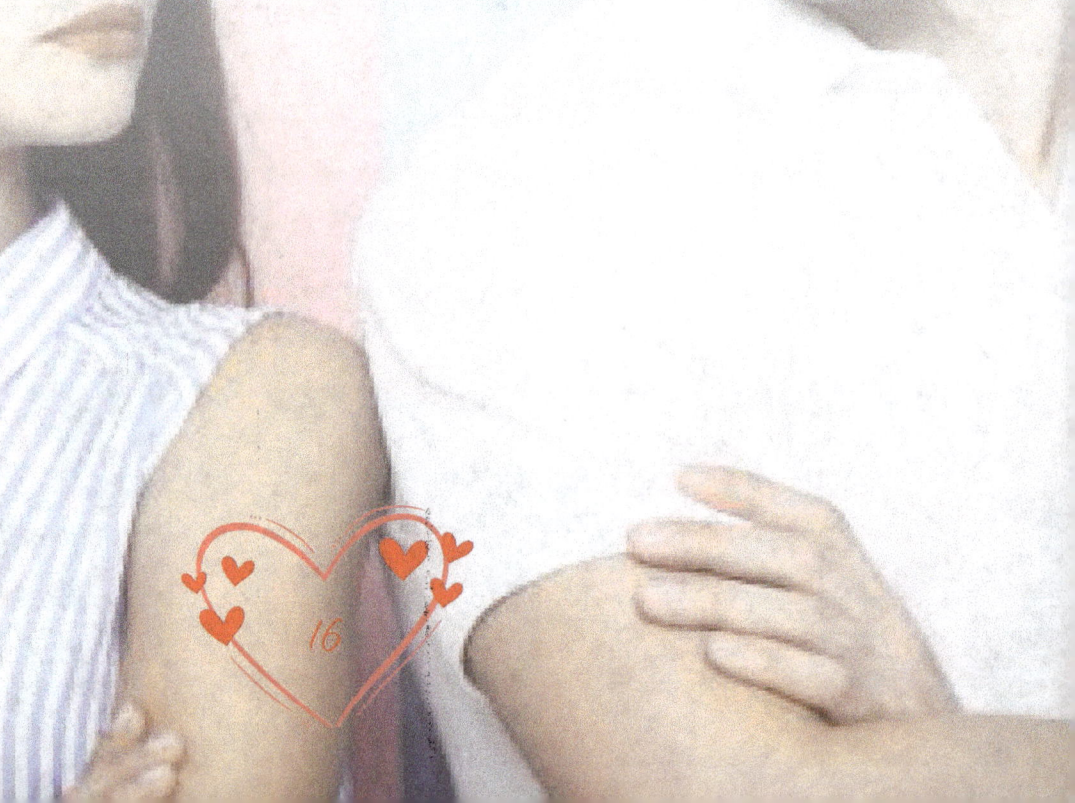

Moments of POETRY

Destiny!

I want to live an honest life
With you,
Believe me woman,
It's all true.
So, many temptations bring lust
It's getting hard to keep the trust.
I keep telling myself
I must not get bust over cheap lust.
I wouldn't know how to live,
If I break your trust.
I know, I'm only a guy
That you gave a try
You know since I met you
I've never told a lie.
You'll always adore me,
I'll never let you cry.
Even at life's hardest moments
I won't give up.
I will always try...
We should stand together
And stand strong forever
So, people will see that
Our love kept us together.
And this is nice?
You don't need to think
About it twice.
If I am fire then your ice,

Moments of POETRY

Destiny!

It's only together
When we look nice.
All those loving moments
Night after night.
Don't you ever say
For each other
We are to be not right.
My life revolves around you
I'm sure I will lose
All my sounds without you
I've never felt better
Apart from that time
I wrote you that love letter,
Telling you no one
Can love you better.
Then you made the call
Which made my dreams come true
I'll be lost without
You in this world
Loving you is all
I want to do.
Loving you is all
I live for.

Moments of POETRY

Be Mine!

Life has so many issues.
Every time you have a problem
All you do is waste tissues,
After crying your eyes over
Materialistic issues.
When life is hard, give it a try.
It's better than doing nothing
But having a cry
Even when I ask you,
You can't explain why?
Every time
I see your lips move
I think: here comes
Another lie.
Can't you be honest too?
Just give it a try!
You say you love me
Or was it all a lie.
If I am what you want
Don't ever drop another tear,
Living your life in fear.
I'm here next to you,
Wanting you to be you.
You're the only one
I ever found to be true.
Hope you truly understand
How much I care for you

Moments of POETRY

Be Mine!

From the first day we met.
Hope there is nothing in your heart,
Which you regret
Or I will forever punish
Myself.
Never forget —
Holding it
As the biggest regret
In my life,
I want you to know
How much more I need you
In my life,
Needing you to
Be my wife.
It's only around you
I truly feel alive

Moments of POETRY

Baby oh my Baby

Baby oh my baby,
Let's sit and talk,
Maybe in a bit we can get up
And take a walk
On the grass
Maintaining our class,
Drinking
The champagne out of the bottle
Forgetting the glass.
After moments of staying away
All I do is sit and pray
That to get to you
My Lord
Will show me the way
I hope we never lose each other
Because I wouldn't know what to still be living
My life but without a clue.
Don't want to let you go
Want to stick to you like glue
Never let go: what we share is true
Only if you can understand
How much you mean to me.
It's been so long since we last spoke
I know how it goes
Hopefully it will only get better as only God knows
What I feel for you is all I try to show.
Need you by my side
Because when you are with me girl
My inner spirit can't hide.

Moments of POETRY

Explanation

I'm neither good nor bad
It is only when I don't get to see you
That I feel sad.
Or am I just getting punished for something bad.
You're the only one I ever had
Separating us now, I wonder who will be glad.
You're my baby mama
And I'm your baby dad.
Want to give our child
Everything I never had
So that he can be proud of his dad.
I promise,
I'll never cheat on you with your best friend
And tell you a lie.
I'll give up and try
So that our kids never have to cry
Asking mamma what sort of guy was I.
Then you having to lie, just because
You never gave me that one chance to try.
All humans make mistakes
Unlike others I'll do whatever it takes

Moments of POETRY

Explanation

To make up and wakeup.
As God is looking from above
Don't torture me anymore.
I'm sorry, never want you to worry
When it's all good I'll cook you a curry.
Take things slow
It's our life we are living, not a show.
Don't want anyone to know
What's going on between us anymore.
For the world we are going to live
Our life behind a closed door.
As we try to live
I'll hope one day I do something
So that you can forgive me, my wife.
I need you with me to get anywhere in this life.

Moments of POETRY

Desires

People live life in desires
Like loose ends on electrical wires.
Making things bad like crazy fires
Stop hiding the truth and becoming liars.
The world would be a better place
If we were all tryers.
There is no point going for war
When you can go for love.
What answer are you going to give?
To the One Lord
We all know
He is watching from above.
Do what you want to do
When you want to do
How you want to do.
Your style has got to be true
All my life,
I never met a girl like you.
Happy, you're rare
Loving qualities of companionship

Moments of POETRY

Desires

Is it the gift from My Lord?
Calling you championship
If I was told to love again
It's something I can't do,
As love was the only thing,
I ever saved for you.
Don't you ever worry
Or drop a tear
Don't ever live your life
In fear.
One thing that should be
Crystal clear
Is that when it comes to you
I'm always here.
Losing you remains my only fear
Don't walk away.
You walking into my life,
Was like an
Answered prayer
This kept me here!

Moments of POETRY

Fine!

Every time I look at you
and back with you
The only thing
I realize
you are getting more finer
You got me here like
Romeo
Dropping line after line.
The only intention
For me now is
Making you mine,
I love you girl
Want you
To love me back
Sing me all the time
Like everyone's Favorite track
I'm here in your life
To create an impact
So, you realize

Moments of POETRY

Fine!

That as I look
Deep in your eyes
I'm not like other guys.
Would never tell you lies
Because when you find out
You would be upset
And ask me why? After, why?
Regretting
Who do you chose
To be
Your guy?
Please baby don't do this,
Don't cry
Seeing you upset makes
Me want to die.
This is not a lie!
To earn your love again
Till eternity
I will try...

Moments of POETRY

Married Man!

I'm a married man
Who is finding it hard to be good.
Even though I know I should.
Everything around me
Is not what I need.
Just filth and greed
It's hard to be faithful.
As to much bad news
But if I make a mistake
I want you to know
Choose and would never want to lose
Could never walk away from you even if you refuse
All the love we share. Be aware.
Do not walk away every time something is going wrong.
Turn to God & pray
That we stay together.

Moments of POETRY

Married Man!

Every day I'm sure the Almighty God

Will show you the way.

We are his creation just like fire and ice

Only together

Baby we look nice.

Everything else may be lust but

From the first instance you got my trust along with love

I'm sure you're a blessing in disguise.

For I am sent from above.

You are not just my love but also my soul mate

I'm sure if we are together

Forever the results will be neat.

Moments of POETRY

Diamonds

Diamonds are rare —
Whoever gets one
Don't want to share
Even if they truly care.
Just like the way you came into my life
Relationship are sharp like the edge of a sharp knife
I want to drop down to one knee
And ask you if you will be mine
Till eternity
As there's more to you
Than just
Your pretty smile
It brings out the best of me
More than just once in a while.
I will do whatever it takes
To maintain your smile
Want to make a future
With you in it
If I have that
Everything else
In life I'm sure
I will win it.

Moments of POETRY

Slow Down

Slowly, slowly I will work on
Your heart
Get to know and understand
Each and every part.
As for your simple smile
What a state of art
I'm over the moon
Because this isn't the end
It's surely the start.
Day and night
I won't let you out of
My sight
Want to start kissing you
From early morning
Till late Night
When it comes to you,
I don't think I
Will hesitate
Cause when you look at reality,
We can relate.

Moments of POETRY

Slow Down

You're my perfect soul mate.
Sorry for leaving it so late.
I'm fun thinking of joining
You in the sun
Even if it starts to rain
To get to you
I don't mind going through pain
I would hurry because I would never
Want you to worry.

I'm sure that I and you
Are feeling 100% sure.
For all my heart problems,
You're the only cure.
Let me touch
You and tease you.
If life ever gets hard,
I will do everything
To ease you
Don't ever want you
Thinking this is all a lie
Give me credit girl,

Moments of POETRY

Slow Down

At least, I gave it a try.
Looking into your eyes
Wanting you to realize that
Everything before you
Which I enjoyed
I have now
Sacrificed!

Moments of POETRY

Artistic

Like a clear canvas of art
Girl I have wanted you
From the start.
If we are two different people
Hope God never does us apart
It's like separating
The body from the heart
How am I supposed to beat?
You're the only one
I have ever wanted to meet.
Throwing roses
At your feet
Opening my arms
When you show up
To greet
Hope one day
You will be mine
To keep!

Moments of POETRY

CPR

Kiss of life
Is all I want from you,
As the feeling has never been
So pure
My heart has never been
So sure
Never before you did I
Want to offer my
Love and companionship
Celebrating like
I'm winning my first championship
You are the one I'm truly missing
Want to let you know
You're the one for me
Want to be holding and kissing,
Every time you go away
I sit and miss.
I want you to
Remember this —
Only together we look Kris.
Let me hold you in
My arms
Keeping you away from all
The harm

Moments of POETRY

Still Lonely

It's so sad waking up lonely
Finding yourself in bed only.
Love to give you a hug, making love
To you in front of the coal fire,
On the rug.
Baby, I'm your lover
Stop thinking of me as a thug.
I'm real baby, not materialistic.
Not a fool,
I know only when I'm with you
I feel cool
It's like that good feeling
After a swim
In the pool or having a Jacuzzi.
Do you remember
The first time we kissed
In the theatre after the movie?

Moments of POETRY

Still Lonely

Come on baby,
This is not the way
I had planned to be in
Your demand
All I'm thinking of is
Being your number one man
If you were just a vehicle
I'll love to be attached.
Even if I was just your
Caravan
Where you can sit and sleep
And maybe mine to keep.
Don't look at this as
Just a saying,
I'm serious about you, so
Don't ever say you thought
I was playing.
Until eternity, is
My heart
Where you ought to
Be staying?

Moments of POETRY

Stop!

Slow down, I can't be running after you
In town;
Even If you want to
Mess around
As much as I want to
Get to know you.
The inner qualities
Within me
Is something I want to show you.
It's only then you will know
What you got.
We only get one chance,
So give it your best shot.
I don't want you to come back
And say I forgot.
Baby, it's true love,
Not something that will rot;
In all your moments
Whether it's good or bad;
Happy or sad
To be all yours;
I'll really be glad,
It's better than leaving you
All alone
To cry to some
Stranger on your phone
I'm still yours
Let's return back to
What we had.

Moments of POETRY

Shy

Don't be shy girl;
Give it a try
That's the only way
You're going to find
Your ideal guy
Don't be playing dumb
Or asking why?
It took me a lot of courage
To try.
I'm here putting everything
On the line
You're the one
I want to refer
As mine
The effect you have
On me
Is better than any
Gig or cig,
Bar or fast car,
Diamonds or jewels.

Moments of POETRY

Shy

As for feelings,
It's something in my heart.
This will rule my heart
As I can't be leaving your side
As it would feel
I'm not doing my part.
Now, at 24
Wanting you even more
5ft 8
Don't want to hesitate
Even if we leave it late
I'm sure only together
We look great.

Moments of POETRY

Realness!

Like a river and lake
It's natural for all humans
To make mistakes.
But I want to give and take
Sitting with you every tea time
Sharing another slice of cake
With a cup of tea
Making all your fantasies
Into my realities
A clash of bodies
Not just personalities
Bringing out
Each other's inner qualities
Everybody can share stories.
But with you
I want to share all realities.
If you answer your phone
Only then
We will both know you're not
Alone

Moments of POETRY

Realness!

Stop being depressed
Hurry and get dressed;
It's not worth being stressed.
So, if you had a bad past
Understand that the negativity will
Fade
Keep taking positive breathes
Everything in your past
Can't last forever
Life itself is a test.
As a human,
Always be fair and give
It your best
Maybe one day
You will be an
Example for the rest.

Moments of POETRY

Cry Hug!

Let me cry
Hold you in my arms
And give it a try.
So, what if life is hard
And we are far apart.
No matter what
You are all over
My mind and heart
Nothing but death
Can do us apart
Even to heaven
When you win
The race
No matter what
Save me a place
Without you
I'll be like a
Cat
In a rat race!

Moments of POETRY

1st Time!

The first time I saw you
Was from a distance.
I couldn't help
But to give you my heart
In the first instance.
You are special and true
No matter what,
I can't get enough
of you
You're the secret behind
My smile
The improvement needed in
My style
I haven't felt this Amazing
In a while
Give me your heart, now
I'll keep it safe
And protected.
You're the one
My heart
Selected.

Moments of POETRY

Belonging!

Even though we belong together
I'm sitting far away from you
Wishing you were here
Next to my side.
Or chilling with me
In my ride
Coming after you
Every time you go
To hide
The life we live
Surely is wild
Always wanted you
To have my child —
Son or daughter
Sharing a relationship
As pure as water
Crystal clean
Hope God bless us even more
Making us a team,
I'll be your King
If you promise
To be my Queen.

Moments of POETRY

Sing Along!

I sing, song after song
Want you to
Know
I will never do you
Wrong
Always want to get along
Making our relationship
Strong.
Never walk away baby
Blaming me for your insecurities
I'm here to stay and pray
That I can be with you
Each and every day
Whether we are on
A high or a low
Just want to let you know
That you're the one
For me
So, I can never
Let you go.

Moments of POETRY

Workplace!

It all started
When I came to your
Work place
Noticing your pretty smile
Along with
Beautiful face,
I was lost for
Words.
In just a moment I felt some
Tension
First time in my life
My feelings,
I couldn't mention
Just like school days —Detention

Moments of POETRY

Workplace

I want to be left behind
To give you my 100% attention
I don't really know you and
You already mean
The world to me.
You are an amazing start
To what could complete me.
You're not just a fantasy
Or something for everyone
To see
I believe when
God made you
Even he thought
Of me!

Moments of POETRY

Attention!!

Can't help but to give you my
Attention.
As I noticed your beauty
And have to mention,
I want you right here
By my side
Never live your life
In fear,
I really like the fact that
You're simple.
Couldn't help but to spot
Your dimple
On the cheek I kissed
Whilst your eyes remained closed
I tell you honestly I'm happy
You're the one I choose
You're the one I miss.

Moments of POETRY

Attention!!

We both understand
It's not all about
Kissing and caressing.
That's why I do my part
Stopping you from
Stressing
In our relationship,
We can do it all
The Lord gave me you
As a
Blessing.

Moments of POETRY

Charmer Drama!

You look at me as a charmer
I know I filled your life
With unplanned drama,
Even though it wasn't what
Was intended
Life without you is no fun
It's like having the
Summer season
With no sun.
Feel like an
Empty gun
So, forget the
Rapid fire.
You're the one
I want
And truly admire.
My feelings are real

Moments of POETRY

Charmer Drama!

You can hire and fire.
Just because
You desire
When you're not there
I get upset.
But every time
I think of you
I know girl
I have nothing to regret.
I question your return
Into my life
Will it be similar?
To the
First time we met.

Moments of POETRY

Angel!

My angel,
I need you to confess.
Without you, my life
Is nothing but a mess.
When you're not with me
All I do is stress.
You don't have to go with
My dress code
All you got to do is come
From your street to my
Area code
Call my name.
I want you sitting
In my heart
Rather than on my bedroom

Moments of POETRY

Angel!

Wall
In a frame
This is love baby
Don't think we are
Playing a game
You're always
Running through my mind
This is serious not just
Bump and grind.
Wherever you look baby,
In front of you;
I'll be there and you
I will find
Only for the
Simple reason that you are
One of a kind.
Even the first time I saw you
On the scene
I thought to myself
All my life,
Where have you been?

Moments of POETRY

Stop Trying!

Stop Trying!
You always say
I don't stop trying,
But the good thing
That happened
To me is to you.
I'm not lying;
The only thing
I'm trying to stop is
My heart from crying.
Without you,
I see myself
Dying bit by bit.
Knowing that
You were crying
Will bring me
Back from dead,

Moments of POETRY

Stop Trying!

Only to be left again
To die
Girl, you know I can't see
You crying
So, stop.
I know even you've been
Lying
If lovers meet in heaven
I'll ask my
Lord to help
Us meet again
For sure!
Hope you don't start denying.

Moments of POETRY

Feelings!

Why do you get scared?
While I'm telling you how I feel.
Doesn't it appeal?
Or don't you believe me.
I know you think
It's not real
Or tell me
What's the deal?
You're holding back
And I'm letting go.
What I feel inside me,
You should honestly know.
Got a lot more
Quality time to show
The way you
Like it.
I've known you long enough
To say "yea",
Baby I know.

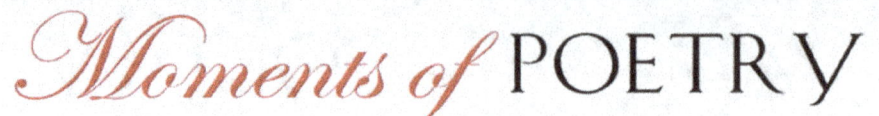

Moments of POETRY

Auto-Phrasing!

Girl you're amazing.
The moment
I saw you my words started
Auto-phrasing
All my life, you're the one
I have been chasing.
Then you started running,
To think we were racing.
Then, I told you to stop,
If you come into my arms.
The world is something in which
We will get to the top.
I want to love you forever,
Non-stop
Just like Pringles,
I can't wait for you to pop....
And never stop.

Moments of POETRY

Amazing!

I am here feeling free
To take out your frustration.
But baby when I ask you,
You got to give me an explanation
To our situation
To avoid any unwanted complications.
My heart shows me indications
You can leave me in pain and
Soak me in the rain.
But whenever it comes to
Making you smile
My style will remain,
Helping you gain
All the love you desire
Because the first time I saw you
All I did was to stop and admire.
Shocked and dazed.
All my feelings in front of me
Damn, I was amazed!

Moments of *POETRY*

Eyes!

Beautiful smile and pretty eyes
Can only be honest.
Would never tell you lies,
I'm sure by now you
Understand.
I'm not like the other guys.
Your smile does wonders
And so, do you.
Everything else in life may be false
But I know you're true.
When the Lord created
Gorgeous people
Like you,
He only created a few.
Now, you sit
Back and admire
My words
Which are true!

Moments of POETRY

Deep!

Thre3dee deeper than a well
A story you can tell.
A fragrance which you would
Love to smell,
Always on your side
Wishing you well
Want to be more than
Just your pride
Nothing cheap
Like a one-night stand.
You're the one for me
You will always be
In demand
Forget the car ride; let's go
Old School.
Hold my hand throughout
The night;
I won't ever let you
Out of sight
You were always
Definite;
I never thought
I might!

Moments of POETRY

Clear Intentions!

Going into the world with
Clear intentions
No one in the world seems
Bothered,
So no need to mention
Every time,
You want to say
How you feel
People
Think your heart
Seeks attention
So, you end up being confused
And ignored
You fall in love thinking,
Everything on my mind
I will now mention
After hearing her story
I want to leave
And just run to another
Dimension...

Moments of POETRY

Small Mind!

Stop thinking with a
Small mind,
Stop wasting your time.
There's more to life than just
Bump and grind.
Yes, you got it right
In the first instance.
I'm definitely one of a kind.
You can't blame me
For the wild thoughts running
Through your mind.
You can seek
But I will only reveal
What I need to
Once I think it's time for you
To Find!

Moments of POETRY

Shivers!

Holding you in my arms
Making you shiver
Every wild thought of yours
You never know
When I might
Consider.
From morning to Mid-day
Making love in every passionate way
A plan to stay together
Making love forever,
Wrapping you in my arms
In every bad weather.

Moments of POETRY

Lusty Love

Love and lust both start
With commitment and trust
Until one day you get bust.
How do you tell?
Someone is fake or real
How you suppose to
Comeback after making
A mistake
Because in reality
You don't
Always get an
Opportunity to retake
It's not always easy
To drift like a piece of cake
So, think and consider
Your lust
Is it really worth losing
The one
Who always gave you Love?
Along with her all.
Start with an apology on the
Next call.

Moments of POETRY

To My Loving Mum

Mother, oh mother!
In this world, I have seen a lot
But no one other
Than my mother
You gave me blessings
As a sister and a brother
I love you my mother.
Just to let you know —
I cannot replace you
In this life of mine.
As there is no other,
You are always there
To share every fear
Still, it's sweet
How you don't let
Me shed a tear?
Mum I ...will always love you
Want you to know
I'm here...
. To my loving mum

Moments of POETRY

Pleasuring Pain

Just like pleasure and pain
Want you to share all of them
Wild thoughts of you are running
Through my brain
Without you, going insane
Like snakes on plain
I want your love all over me now.
Come on, pour on me like rain
Whatever you do don't forget to
Hollaback
Remember my name
I want to do a lot more to you
Than just putting my picture
In your frame,

Moments of POETRY

I Look

The first time I saw you
I looked and was amazed.
Girl. You left me in a daze
Looking deep into your eyes,
They were like a crystal maze.
Since then, I'm having problems
I can't look in any other ways
I think about you in my nights
And days
Sometimes, I think
God may have sent you as the
Answer to my prayers.

Moments of POETRY

Perfect Strangers

We are strangers but it's sweet
If you're like a sound track.
I'll love to be your beat,
Like two ends of a river.
Just hope one day we meet
I'll rise to my feet just to
Open my arms and greet.
Because you're not typical,
Not someone who I can replace.
With any one from the street.
Results can be neat.
Memories can be sweet
I'll be a heart if you promise
To be my beat.

Moments of POETRY

Attention!

Can't help but to give you my
Attention.
As I noticed your beauty
And I have to mention.
If we were like school kids
I love to be left behind with you
In detention.
So that time after time I can mention.
On your cheek you have a dimple
Which I want to kiss
Whilst holding you in my arms
And whispering
In your ear, "Baby you are the one I miss.
And will never diss."
I understand it's not all about
Kissing and caressing,
That's why I do my part.
And try to prevent you from
Stressing in our relationship
We can do with every blessing.

Trust-tactic

Never break a girl's trust.
Don't give out her number
And show her your lust
It's bad enough.
You hurt her for everything
She ever felt.
It's a bit sad to know
You were only after her body
And wealth.
Stop going all materialistic;
Don't break her trust.
It's not fair to be so mistreated
And cheated
Show her in love how one should
Be appreciated,
Not hated.
Together equated;
No Egos
Or being egotistic
You can now try to be realistic.

Moments of POETRY

Guy Fact!

When a guy is honest and
Pouring his heart out
You say he is OK but you
Prefer him at the start.
Is it because he only gave you
Attention?
And all his time,
You treated him bad
Making him feel like he has
Committed a crime.
Only with you
He wanted to do his
Time
Stop being a gold digger
Thinking about just yourself.
Love should be a two-way thing
Want you to be more
Than Everything
I shouldn't have to be
Suffering!

Moments of POETRY

Needs!

Love you like diamonds
And jewels.
Don't want anyone to think
Of us as fools.
Want to appreciate you
Like a workman with his tools.
Don't do us apart;
You were made for me.
Call it sizzle or hammer
All I want you to do
Is being my baby mamma.
Promise to fill your life
With thriller,
Romance, suspense and
Drama

Moments of POETRY

Confession!

I think it's time to confess and
Get all this off my chest.
For us to be together
I will always do my best.
Nothing like the rest,
You can always put
Me to the test
If you got problems
I'm sure the cure
Is something I can suggest?
I'm not just staying or playing
Want you in my arms,
I have saved you a place
In my heart
Where I want you to be
Staying

Moments of POETRY

Moments

Moment's together, days apart
Don't waste a tear over someone who
Wasn't worth it from the start.
Don't be upset, because you were rejected
Be happy you are free
And can walk away as you weren't
Selected.
It may not be nice
But don't think about it twice.
Throw that idiot
Just like a Board game dice.
Put up your smile on
As you really look
Nice.

Moments of POETRY

Lovers!

Lovers and friends —
Even good things come to an end.
Be yourself and don't
Pretend as you have
Everything to lose
And nothing to gain.
It's your choice
You choose
But when it goes wrong, don't pick
People to blame
Because you were wrong for
Playing a game.
I gave you my love and trust
You threw it back in my
Face as lust.
Tell me how I can ever
Pick you
To trust.

Moments of POETRY

New Years!

Days, hours and moments have passed
Thank the Lord as the
New Year is here at last.
Being generous, kind and loving.
Wishing you the best for
The days coming
We, here, there and everywhere
Diamonds like you are truly rare.
If I said I don't love you
That won't be fair
You are special, not just
An affair
If you were to ever leave me,
I will break down
So, don't you dare...

Moments of POETRY

Snowy times!

Sitting here sulking
About the snow.
I want my baby next to me
So, a good time is something
For sure.
When we were strangers,
I wanted to get to know
You better
That's why I started by
Writing you a love letter
Kissing you on the cheek and
Telling you
I know I can do it better.
I can never forget
Never give her a
Chance to regret
Be happy because you are
Mine from
The moment we met...

Moments of POETRY

Lotion!

Want to be in your arms
Night and day,
Want to do more than
Just sit and play
My heart is the only place
I want you to stay.
I include you in my every thought
And prayers.
Even after a long argument.
I let you have it your way.
Once you leave, you're the one I miss
Can't walk away from this.
Your love got me moving
In a motion,
When my heart pours out
To you in a
New motion!

Moments of POETRY

Returning!

Moments and days away
Come back to me like the
Answer to my prayers.
If I have you, I'll be yours.
I promise no affairs but
Quality times which we can appreciate
We will bring two families
And our hearts together
Just to relate.
Hope I can get further than just being
Your mate.

Moments of POETRY

Self-Beating!

Meeting you was like

Composing a beat.

Holding you in my arms

Made me skip a heartbeat.

I always thought you

Were sweet.

Hope one day destiny brings us

Close so we can meet.

Moments of POETRY

Instructions!

Don't ever want you to go
Don't ever want to lose you,
You were put on earth for my loving.
I didn't just choose you.
I want to go on a cruise with you.
And never would I abuse you
Because you bring out the best in me
You are different;
I can't compare you to the rest
Want to hold you in my arms
So, the Lord can bless.

Moments of POETRY

Only you!

Feeling lonely
Wanting you only.
If only we could be together
Will bring better things definitely
Better than the British weather.
Missing you remember
Me kissing you,
Even in a crowd.
I can never see myself dissing you,
You're gorgeous like a princess.
With your smile
Get rid of my stress
Never before did I confess
Without you my life is
Like a mess.

Moments of POETRY

Illusion!

People's fakeness
People get involved and
Get filled with it
Don't really care for you
Not even a single bit of it.
When you are down
They try to make
You
End Up
Giving in to them —
Saying I quit.
But not me!
I want to get
To the end of it
Even if you walk out of
My life,
Not meaning any of it.
Every single mistake
Is a lesson bigger than any Lake.
You got to learn from every mistake!

Moments of POETRY

Companion!

We chilled day and night
Put each other
From wrong to right.
Best to just walk away.
When left on your mind
Is nothing good to say.
If we were kids, I'm sure
I would have beat you up
When you come out to play.

Moments of POETRY

Fire!

Fire has been burning
Heads have been turning
Still baby, I don't see you learning
Or making progress.
All you ever do is sit and stress
You can't achieve your dreams
And desires sitting next to coal fires.
Anything in life you want, you got
To earn.
From every experience you got
To learn....

Moments of POETRY

Fast Lane!

Enjoying life and chilling
In the fast lane
Get confronted by pleasure and pain.
Cool, I remain
Work like one vanish
When it comes to getting rid
Of the stain
All I want to do is stay on top of my
Game
So, you remember my name
Whilst you are enjoying pleasure
I might show up again, like pain.

Moments of POETRY

Slow Motion!

Living life in a slow motion

Feels like a fish free in the ocean

Chilling deep in the sea.

All I want is you and me

All I want to do is

Start a family tree.

Give me a call if you agree,

Hopefully one day you will be

In my destiny.

Girl, you bring out

The best in me.

Moments of POETRY

Flowing!

Chilling here, coming on a flow
So entertaining.
I could host my own show
Full of comedy and drama.
I'm sure you are
Going to tell my stories
To your girl's
Baby mamma.
She knew, I'm special
More than a charmer
If you are a wild animal,
I'm a farmer.
Do nothing to harm her
Change you with training
Do not worry or start
Any straining
If you're a loss then
There will be nothing
I'll be gaining.

Moments of POETRY

Times!

Moments together and days apart
Why do we have to be so far apart?
My heart is like a plain canvas
You're the art
Always on my mind.
This is more serious than just
Bump and grind.
For sure,
I'm more than just one of a kind
Let me know if you want to
Share those wild thoughts
On your mind

Moments of POETRY

Moon!

Sky is the limit
And even the moon got footprints.
I want to go with you
Like the picture in the frame.
All I want you to do girl is
Remember my name.
Sure, there is going to be allot
Of pleasure
But don't forget the pain.
Cool
Is how I want you to remain?
My love will always grow.
For you
So, all I want to say is
Happy Valentine

Moments of POETRY

Foreign Currency!

Worth more than a dollar
Worth more than a dime.
Like a star, baby
Each and every corner.
I'm going to get to shine
Want you to know I got
Intentions
of making you mine.
Don't look at it just as a line
Or a lie.
It was hard for me to try.
If I don't get you
I might even die.

Moments of POETRY

Roses!

Roses are red and
Violets are blue
Come into my arms baby.
Let me treasure and pleasure you
Day and night
Never will I let you out of my sight
Even when we are going wrong
Baby, I'll put it right.
Want to wish you a
Happy Valentine
Wish till eternity you
Remain mine
Like a star, baby
I want to see you
Shine.

Moments of POETRY

Comeback!

Shall we leave it to destiny?
Or bring it back to you and me?
Because, I want you to be
A part of me each and every day.
Never want you to leave me again
Please stay as you are.
All I ask for
In every prayer is you.
I want to get rid of
Every distance
Giving you all my love
In the first instance,
You won't be let down
That's my guarantee
Because
I want to start ...a family.
Beginning with you & I.
So, stop messing and stop stressing
Come into my arms
Let me carry you like a
Blessing.

Moments of POETRY

Not Lasting!

Me and you look good in the past
But now I'm ashamed because of you.
Baby, we couldn't make it last.
Baby, it was easy for you to leave me
So, what if without you
I go insane
Baby, you moved on and
Left me in your past
You never know when
I might turn up
Like a blast from the past.
Do you think your smile
Will still last?
Karma doesn't let anyone cheat
I'm sure for you
It has its own treat

Moments of POETRY

Changes!

Love changes everything,
Even people.
If you are not going to let me enter
Your heart,
How am I going to play my part?
You're rushing to the end
Whilst I'm only getting
To the start.
Let me kiss and caress
Getting rid of the stress
And making you happy.
With a permanent smile;
It's not temporary.
I want it there
All the while!

Moments of POETRY

Chilling!

Chilling all the time
Chilling all the while.
There is nothing in this world that
I wouldn't do to see you smile.
It's been long since I last saw
You & that pretty face.
It's funny, how in life we run
After material things, just to participate
In the race, when we should instead put all to rest.
I want to be honest, telling you,
You are the best...

Moments of POETRY

After Love!

Chilling here on a Sunday
Thinking about you,
Wondering if you are
Coming out to play.
Or shall inside we stay
Making love on the floor
Or even on the couch.
Let everything rock, baby don't say
Ouch
From minutes to hours
Going to show passion in the
After love shower.
Where the water will be pouring
Only I will be scoring.

Moments of POETRY

Next!

Moving on with the struggles
In life is
So tough and feels like the edge
Of the knife
Or even the next man's
Unfaithful wife.
After making love,
She doing my head and
Pouring out about her life
Saying she is feeling lonely
And how she hurts
Even without money, her fake
Love can't be bought.
Stop for a moment and give
Yourself a thought
How can you demand trust?
When all you have to offer is
Lust!!

Moments of POETRY

Fire flames!

Like a burning fire

It's you I desire.

Hard to control myself

But I still sit back and admire.

You can believe me

Or call me a liar.

But I've always been honest

From the start.

Couldn't help myself but to give

You my heart.

I see you as an empty canvas

May I cover you?

With Art?

Moments of POETRY

Tigress!

Little tigress, come on stop
The stressing.
Come back in my arms
Let me carry on with the
Caressing.
After I finish undressing your body
Get rid of the cover
Because, I want to be deep
Inside more than a lover
Making your body shiver.
Any promise I make to you I will
Certainly deliver.
I may be highly addictive
Don't worry about losing your liver.

Moments of POETRY

Money!

Got to plan my mission
From pennies to pounds.
I wonder who will be around
To show me love and affection.
Who's going to be the one?
For me, who I can offer my protection
Never give you any negligence.
Since you come into my life
It's all perfect, no need for
Any more corrections.

Moments of POETRY

Controversy!

It's not hard to see the start
Of the controversy
That started between you and I.
Did not want us to be apart
from each other's destiny.
I can't believe you just walked away
And forgot me.
Is it because you got a new lover
Or a backup plan?
He doesn't really feel for you!
Hope you understand.
Whilst you thought of him
As your backup plan
All you were to him was
A one-night stand.

Moments of POETRY

Vanish!

Whenever I make time for you,
You vanish.
I'm talking straight forward English
Why are you ignoring me?
Like you're not, understanding me
I'm not speaking Spanish
What's wrong with you? Pay attention.
Or is there something your parents
Forgot to mention?
As you look at everything
In a different dimension
Meeting you in the future
Will definitely be my
New prevention
Hope you ...understand
That the paths differ?
Hope you're cool.
No longer will
I want you to take me
For a fool.

Moments of POETRY

Tears!

Don't cry
Don't let anyone lie.
All you got to do
Is pull yourself together
And stop all this drama because
Of a guy
Why put yourself through the pain
When all he is doing is playing a game
Get rid of him like he is a stain.

Moments of POETRY

My prayers!

Chilling in the day
Chilling in the night.
How do you define?
Wrong from right.
Don't ever want you
Out of my sight
As my world goes upside down
Every time you get busy.
It's not material
I want as pounds and cars,
For eternity won't be around.
I only always want to wake up to
That sexy voice of yours
What a sound!
If you ever need me
I'm only a call away
My Lord understands...
It's you for whom I pray.

Moments of POETRY

Big Ben

Back again
Chilling in the city with my friend,
The Big Ben
He says tick and I say tock.
We are chilling like everyday
All around the clock
For some moments, we stop and are in shock
For others whilst we go clubbing
Dancing to rock
Catching the tube or underground
But still me, I get around
In the morning or at night
London city Seems Alright!

Moments of POETRY

Confirm!

You got to admit
The relationship we share is rare.
You can tell anyone
In the world about it
And say we truly care.
Also, we appreciate
The fact that it's only
Together we look great.
I feel for you strongly,
Don't want you to hesitate.
If you also feel for me strongly,
Tell me how we can relate.
I got to admit,
It's quite shocking.
Ever since you
Have been in my life,
It's all been rocking.
Just don't ever say
It's the wrong door
I'm knocking.

Moments of POETRY

The Past!

I never knew how to rap
All I ever did was sit in the crowd and clap
Until I realized that it's time
To bring out my desire.
Getting my point across
Like a spreading wildfire,
Got a journey from a penny to a pound.
I wonder when I am going to get crowned.
Without my fortunate lady.
I'm incomplete;
I need her here to help
Me compose a beat.
Let's take the bump to the grind
Like a bad credit card
Transaction don't you
Decline…

Moments of POETRY

Soul Mate

It was like within you girl

I found my soul mate.

It was like you were taken

From my heart and mind

Then planted on earth.

My love is yours

As that's

What you're worth.

Moments of POETRY

Belief!

I stand, I drop
I have a strong belief one day
I'll make it to the top.
Got my faith in the Lord
Believing I'm always being watched.
Trying to do right
When all I ever see is wrong.
Why can't everybody in the world
just get along?
Kids crying, adults lying,
Old people die. I am sick of this!
Got to stop people from dying.
All my fellow humans,
I'm here on call
Trying to remove your blindfold.

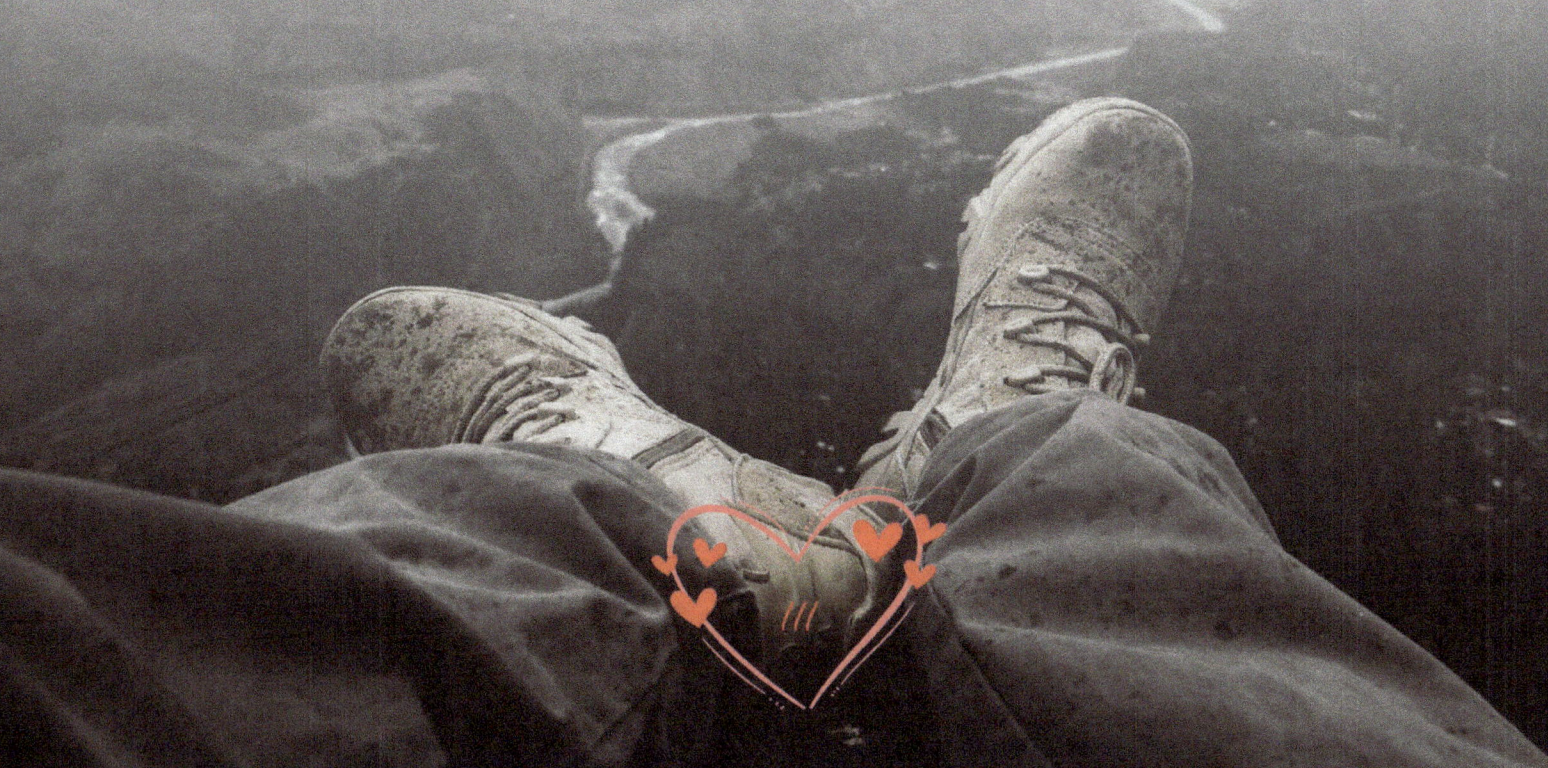

Moments of POETRY

Money!!

Honey, money isn't funny
One minute you got it
The next it's gone.
When you need someone
To love and hold
Your money isn't the one.
Snap out and realize
That it's love you're looking
For, and not a materialistic guy.
Be yourself,
And stop living a life that is a lie,
All of this just to impress a guy?
Be honest,
Is it worth it?
Because the last time we
Spoke you seemed hurt.
Didn't want to say much
Apart from "I miss your touch."
And in this life baby
I appreciate you very much...

Moments of POETRY

Let Down!

People let you down
Over and over again.
They stab you in the back and still
Say they are your friend and
Truly care even though you know
Its non-existent.
Being all rare, in this life
I have loads of problems.
Is it fair!
Why am I crying my heart out
Like you really care?

Moments of POETRY

Train!

Trying to sit peacefully
On a train,
All my problems follow and run
Through my brain.
It feels like I'm going insane,
I feel lied to and misguided.
Now, my feelings
I chose to hide.
As for people in this world
Take you for a ride.
I feel the stress, is there more
To life than this mess.

Moments of POETRY

Last Kiss!

It's been a long time since
I gave you my last kiss.
But want you to know
That it's our special moments
Which I truly miss.
Wish you were here
So, I can truly kiss and caress;
Making love to your heavenly body.
Say God bless.
Not giving a reason to stress,
You're different from the rest.
I want you back,
I want to keep you always,
Close to my chest
Always on like
My Favorite soundtrack.
As for you girl,
You made an impact
Can't stay without you now
Girl, that's a fact.

Moments of POETRY

Wrong & Right!

If I'm wrong and you're right
I promise to sort myself out before
The end of the night.
You're not only my need
But what I want.
You're my hottest desire
You're what I truly admire.
Your beauty can get chemistry
To start between us like a fire.
I'm writing this poem so that
When you read, you are going to say,
I didn't know I had this effect on him!
But I truly want you to be my destiny
As you bring out the best in me.

Moments of POETRY

So Wrong yet So right?

It's so wrong yet so right,
It's so wrong yet so right,
I know I shouldn't be committing
To anyone
But baby in my current relationship
The love is gone.
So, I was out messing until
I met you.
Now, all I want to do is confess
I never found anyone so true.
Can't believe it all started off
With chocolate moments which
You loved.
As you're the one
To whom I presented them
Every day another loving moment
Was granted too.

Moments of POETRY

A thought

Before I met you girl
You were like a thought
Running through
My mind.
It wasn't only till you entered
My life
I realized you're the love
I've always searched for.
Within you girl
I only find everything.

Moments of POETRY

Unconditional

You appreciate my unconditional love
As it's all for you.
I can't believe the situation we are in.
One day,
If you leave, what am I to do?
I call you my girl and my soul mate.
Girl, when I'm in pain
You're the only one
That makes me at ease.
You always can relate.
I love you the most
Even though we haven't made love.
As for me, girl your happiness
Is a lot more than a push and a shove.

Moments of POETRY

Living it

Every day, I live with someone

But still belong to you.

In this life, I live with pain.

Every moment

I'm taken away from you.

All the time,

I've been committed and still lonely.

You're the one

My angel who I now need

My only wish is taking

Forward or backwards

The hands of time

Where I make a time where together

We live on the same

Timeline.

We will live forever —

Your smile girl is what

I treasure.

Moments of POETRY

Spider

I'm not spider man or Peter Parker
But I promise to brighten your world.
Don't let go of my hand.
As everything surrounding
Me goes darker
Can't believe you put your
Name all over my heart
Without a pen
Or marker.

Moments of POETRY

Sleeping Pills

I struggle to sleep
Unless I speak to you at night.
Every day without you
Become a struggle and fight.
Even my doctor says without you
I can't be alright...
God is putting our love to test
Where we can only support
Each other for the best
I know I can't forget you
Even if I forget
The rest...
Can't let go of family honor
So, I'm going to
Sacrifice my dream
Too bad, along
With my dream
I may lose my love
And my Queen!

Moments of POETRY

Lonely, Lonely

Lonely days and lonely nights
Everything feels wrong
Nothing seems right.
Every day has become a struggle
With every day comes a new fight
All I know is that it gets harder
When you're out of sight
Without you how am
I going to reach the greatest height.
I no longer feel good.
We created romance
Over a certain amount of time
When you and I
Together spend loads of time...

Moments of POETRY

Nation

Tsunamis, Tornados and Hurricanes
Keep coming back
The Corona Pandemic
Making everyone lose track
How do we
Hold on to
Our one nation
The love we share
Can't be going out
of equation.
Don't ever give up appreciation.
As we stand as
One nation
Before any color or race.
Support the ones
That need love
Forget the paper chase.
At the time of need
Who do we really
Have indeed?
The World is at distance
Behind its face covering.
Even the BBC in trouble
For what it's not been properly
Covering!

Moments of POETRY

Yesterday

He doesn't know me but
My dreams have become his reality.
She once was known as my love
Actually, A real specialty.
When I found out that you took her
Away from me I found it
Brutality!

Moments of POETRY

Confession

You're beautiful,
You're so amazing
Even my words start auto-phrasing.
Check it
We are so hot together;
I wonder —
Why we are not
Together?
I want to get inside you like
A seed in a pot
Never between us
Will the love stop!

Moments of POETRY

Awaiting

I wait for you all day
I wait for you all night.
Apart from you girl
I can never find
My miss right.
Jlo fan;
You use to love Jlo.
Always telling me your love
Don't cost a thing...
But don't you worry
I've paid the price
Since you left
I haven't stopped suffering.

Moments of POETRY

My Lady

My lady, the true one
My one in a million.
Its funny girl but you're not
Just any civilian.
She found me when she
Was looking for love and affection
Forever I can be hers.
Offering her
My love and protection

Moments of PoETRY

No Wronging

Never will I do you wrong
So that you don't need to come
Back to make a correction.
Forever,
I will love you girl
Never giving you
'rejection'
You're the best girl
I realized that time
When I was making you
As part
Of my selection

Moments of POETRY

Destiny

Girl, you're the one for me.
You bring out the best in me
Can I call you my destiny?
Don't you ever take away
Yourself from me
You're the one
I want to see every day.
Girl, you're so special
And so true
I'm gladly in love
Were stuck together
Like glue.
I love you baby.
I'm so happy
You are my boo

Moments of POETRY

Struggle

My life, my journey,
My struggle and my money.
Can't make nothing without you Honey,
In this lifetime everyone is serious
No one laughs, no one smiles.
To achieve a smile, you are
Running for miles...
My life; full of pain,
My journey never ending.
I'm for real no pretending
Want everyone to smile.
Even if it means
It's my ending.

Moments of POETRY

Blessed

All I ever asked for was a companion
Which they took away from me.
Saying, I can't have it.
I'm no champion, so I can't
Have you as my success.
Without you my life
Remains a mess.
Still, not going to give up,
My faith
Is in the Lord
Sharp like a sword.
Lord, please help me
Put my problems
To rest
I don't believe in anyone
But the One Lord,
Just got to confess

Moments of POETRY

My Way

Everyone's living
Only if we can.
Let's all give each other a thought,
No matter
What race or color.
Let's always be there for
Each Other,
Understanding our values
And respecting each other's
Views
Go around to everyone
Don't just tag along
To join a queue.

Moments of POETRY

Hard Times!

It is funny when you got problems
Feeling down.
No one wants to be there,
No one is ever around.
I just feel like a coffin,
Going deeper
Into the ground.
I want everyone to be
Happy.
Speaking their mind
Why is it that
People think this is just a
Waste of time.
I've always admired you
And always thought you were
Fine
Pitying one's lifetime is not enough
Everyone can be loving
Really, why act to be tough.

Moments of POETRY

Desires

Man can admire,
Man can desire.
You're so beautiful
You can put on a fire.
You're the one I require
So, don't call me a liar.
You are one of a kind
Always on my mind
It's more than just
Bump and grind.
It's a soul mate I'm
Trying to find
Hope like me
You're happy.
We met
And there's nothing
I hope you ever
Have to regret.
My target is set,
Going to give
You miracles
You won't forget.

Moments of POETRY

Raining

Sitting here, I watch the rain.
It's like the first time
You walked away
I stayed in pain and
Went insane
You left me like I was nothing
More than a stain,
That will go away.
I'm forever
Baby I'm here to stay and
Love you in every way,
Every day
I know you're not a
Gold digger
But for you I have
Been digging gold
Together let's grow old and grey
Forever, I want you
In this heart to stay!

Moments of POETRY

Forever...

Forever want you
In my arms to hold
It's funny how you and I
Came together.
Now, you got me wondering
If in this lifetime
We can be together
As losing you mean gaining
Pain.
I always want you to
Remember, that I
Want you to share
My family name.
I could never play you
As this isn't a game.
I want you only,
Now forget money
And fame.

Stars

Want to be with you like the
Stars in the sky.
Don't be shy
You never know.
In the days to come
I could be your guy.
All you got to do is to support
Me and try
As from the start baby
The one thing
I can't face you
With is a lie.
Want to wake up next to you
Every day,
So, don't you ever kiss me,
Goodbye.
You're the one in my heart
You're the one in my mind.
Had to search all my life
Until before my eyes
It's you I find.

Moments of POETRY

Quote

Quote me, and I quote you,
You wrote me and I wrote you.
You thought about me and
I thought about you.
Even when you don't
Think about me
I still think about you.
I can't believe a miracle like you
Could be so true
Damn baby,
I'm so into you.

Moments of POETRY

Minutes to hours

Minute to hours
No longer will I try
Making you feel good
With chocolate & flowers.
I promise to be around you forever
Starting from minutes to hours.

Moments of POETRY

Time to Go

Just leaving your city
I didn't know what to say.
Apart from it hurts
To walk away as I see emotions running
Through your eyes.
It was hard to walk away
So much to say but
I still couldn't say a word.
Stampede in the station
Your heart was the only voice
I heard.
My angel, my baby
Without you I'm going crazy
Losing my Focus.
A lot of lovers getting separated
For the week
Just like us.

Moments of POETRY

V day

Thinking of you
On Valentines.
Thinking about all
Our special times.
Now, distance that has increased
With time it hurts to stay away.
Why were lovers put apart?
Why would you want to
Torture my heart?
It's a day for lovers and I want to
Be deep with you
Under covers.
I understand,
I'm not your Valentine
But, I need you to understand that
I want you to be mine.
Girl, never decline.
As from the first time
I laid an eye on you
I thought only together
We would be fine.

Moments of POETRY

Chance

Sweet, sensible and irresistible
I need
You in this life baby
Just to be comfortable.
Looking into your pretty eyes
Makes me wonder
How do I not get hypnotized?
As you is one of a kind
From the first time I saw you girl
You have been playing on my mind.
Where do I find you?
How can I make you my boo?
It's always nice to
See you smile.
It's the best thing
I find
From mile to mile
Want to keep you forever
As a part of my style even from
A distance
In the first instance,
I wanted to be in your arms
So, I can dance.
Hope a day will come
When I will get the chance?

Moments of POETRY

A Mum

A mother can be young or old.
Mother, I know
Your heart could never get cold.
It's like a deep story
Which still isn't been told.
Everybody is still living
Behind a blindfold
As she's still there
To help her babies in their struggles
Kissing her babies
Every night and keeping
Them away from
Troubles!

Moments of POETRY

The Plan

What I'm planning is a lot
Deeper than romance.
Let's make real love as now it's
Your chance.
Forget techno,
Forget the trance
Me and you
Baby, you have good enough
Reason to dance
Get back on your feet
And shake your booty
To my beat
Every memory from here baby is
Going to be sweet
I can't lose you as I'll be lost
Need your love forever.
At any deal or any cost
I'll find you baby
No matter
Even if it is from
This moment that
I become lost.
Realize, I'm falling in love babe
Deep in your pretty eyes
How do I not get myself
Hypnotized...?

Moments of POETRY

Beliefs

I stand I drop
I have a strong belief one day
I will make it to the top.
Got my faith in the Lord
I believe I'm always being watched
Trying to do it right.
When all I ever see is wrong
Why can't everyone in the world
Just get along?
United we stand divided we fall
Come on fellow humans
Stay on call...

Moments of POETRY

Statement

Cheat and lie
Would you give up on me?
Or support my condition
As I try.
Heal me with your love
Forever being my one
That will never deny.
No longer can we be lovers
But this doesn't have to
Be the end.
I'm always here to welcome you
With open arms
As my love won't
End...

Moments of POETRY

Make Up

You take her to the beauticians
Trying to make her look nice.
Have you ever considered my Love?
You didn't even
Think twice....
You haven't got to
Fix your makeup.
Just got to understand
You left the one who loves
You.
After that break up
Come around
To my place
That's where you need to
Really make up.

Moments of POETRY

Companion

Beautiful day not feeling

The best,

Want to be with my special friend.

It's something I had to confess

Want to be your friend,

Forever taking away your stress.

Anything that comes out my mouth, she be

Like awe bless.

I'm always here to support you baby,

And keep you away from the mess.

I feel special and good

When in me you invest

Your trust

You can try pushing me away

But I can't as your love

Is a must

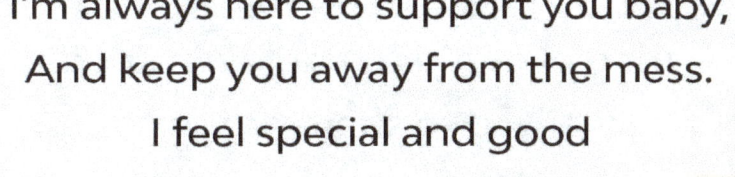

Moments of POETRY

I lie

Girl, I know our relationship
Started off with a lie.
After you got my honesty girl
You know forever
I wanted to make you
Happy.
At least, I know I try to
Fall in love with you the first time.
When I lost,
I tried everything and even cried.
I wanted to share the truth
With the world
But instead I get denied.
It's not always easy to explain my situation
I couldn't even get my soul mate to stay.
Girl, I talk to the Lord, every time
I mention you in every prayer,
Hope forever you stay the same.
In this journey called love,
I can't believe
The amount of pain.
No matter what, don't forget my name
You've been running through my heart as
I ignore my brain...

Moments of POETRY

You left me

Time after time, we kept getting together.
Too bad, every time we were
Split apart.
Don't know when and how
I just gave you my heart.
In this life of mine
I always wanted you around
To play your part
I just want you to know,
I don't hate you one bit
As you're a blessing
For me sent from above.
In this life of mine,
I call you my love.
Too bad, destiny could
No longer keep us together.
Every memory I shared with you
I treasure.
Only days so much love
How will any one measure.

Moments of POETRY

Secret

I'm a married man
Who doesn't know?
The future plan
Just not happy I guess,
Coming out to the world
To find some real love
And shake away the stress.
I found my soul mate
After getting married
I couldn't keep her as
Happiness
Was never something I
Carried
She is a special girl with love
She fills my world,
So special, so rare.
When she is angry
She can be sarcastic
Like she doesn't care
But whenever I was down,
She was always
There.

Moments of POETRY

Still in love

Still love her even though it's been
A long time.
Want you to understand this
Isn't just my words
The thoughts are also mine.
I'm sorry girl, we couldn't complete
Our Love stories.
For me girl, you were the only real glory,
Too bad it had to end.
You really love me so much that
You couldn't even be my friend.
I remember
The first time you entered my life
I wanted to commit to you,
Immediately making you my wife
But, I couldn't as I've already committed
To my parents' wishes
You're the one
I would do anything for.
Even your late-night dishes,
Girl I will love you forever.
Even though nobody understands,
Hope destiny puts us together hand in hand.
As you've always been in demand so loving so real.
I'm sorry girl: I'm not a part of your final deal.
The love I carry in my heart
For you, too bad I could never reveal....

The challenge

Four months exactly
From start to end.
Too bad you couldn't
Be yourself to
Accept the challenge.
You told me you knew
What was on the line?
You told me you knew a way
In which I would be yours,
And you would remain mine.
But don't worry, I already
Know you were lying.
You chose to remove me
From your list of
Facebook friends.
Not as easy as yours
Will my love
Come to an end?

Moments of POETRY

Re-negotiate

You may think you're young
Or naïve.
I use to call you my wife
You told me together
we will face every problem
In life
We will face it together but
You walked away.
Have you really found?
Someone else,
Who can treat you better?
Don't care how bad you suffer
With your acne,
Remember, to comfort you
the Lord sent me
I will keep loving you
But you keep leaving.
I would happily
Exchange your tears
With my smile
No matter how much you try
When in love
Sometimes
You have to cry
Changing your style...

Moments of POETRY

Dreaming

Dream within a dream,
All my life
I have been like a baby; where
Have you been?
She cooks, she cleans
She's making my life happen.
Can't believe you are real
Pleased to feel
As I thought I was in a pretty
Dream.
In reality, I can't call you
Nothing but my Queen

Moments of POETRY

Seasonal

Coming around to a new season
I will love you without
Any reason
Always going to try pleasing you,
As you're the one I see myself
Hugging and squeezing.
Come around let me be your keeper.
Between us, there would be no lies
So that no one comes to cheat you.
Must say I feel very happy when
I come to meet you

Moments of POETRY

Memories

So many memories...

So many hard times

As for a true companion

It's hard to find...

Everyone, quick

To look for

A bump,

To be followed by a grind.

What happened to looking

For true love?

Until you manage to search

And find.

I can't forget you

As I don't need to rewind time.

I love you so much

That you are running through

My heart and mind...

Moments of POETRY

Happiness

Be happy no matter what...
Because the pain,
Anger and drama
Are never going to stop...
Don't get intimidated
By seeing a tall mountain
As only true belief will
Take you to the top...
The love we share should
Never stop...
All my loved ones in life
I'm happy you guys
Are what I got...
To inspire me and truly
Motivate...
I may be hurting but it's never
...too late...
If you didn't know
It's easier to
Love than
It is to hate....

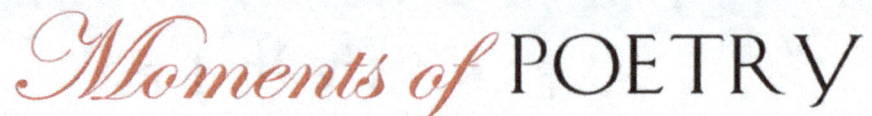

Rhythms

Always remember
Like drum and bass guitars,
I'll be getting all up in your face
It's all about love.
So, don't let anyone bring you down
because of your skin color or race.
As you know,
They are only going to be a lost case.
Be happy no matter your condition
The Lord will always bless you
With a true companion
That will always be around.
So, don't you let anyone
Bring you down...

Moments of POETRY

End

All good things come to an end
No longer can I
Call you girlfriend.
As every single path we had
You brought to an end...
I'm your lover,
Why am I getting treated
Like an offender?
As everything we share is true...
Life may have so much to offer
But I only want you...

Moments of POETRY

Expressing.

Expressing and pouring

Out every emotion

No longer

Can we slow down the motion?

If you remember, that chaos

They call tsunami

Came from the ocean...

Pain and rain can get

You all over.

Every time, you feel like you're

Done...

Remember, it's only

Time to start over

As tougher times have

Gone...

Moments of POETRY

Life

In my life I've made
Some promises
Which I now need to deliver...
Hoping I get the opportunity
I waited for
As no longer can
I cry a river...
Every night I think about that
Special someone.
When it's got cold
I shiver...
Then, I remember
That harsh truth in life
That is not everything
We can get to deliver...
Only you can stop your heart
From crying that river,

Moments of POETRY

Wish

It's nice to see people like
What I say...
Let's just hope in this journey
We call life
Together forever
We stay...
As I ask the Lord
To help the nation
When I pray...
Happiness you carry within
Yourself don't
Forget to give
A bit out every day...

Moments of POETRY

Every day

Every day
There's one of us out there
Ready to fall...
As the one he waited for
Never came around to call...
People are getting hurt
Instead of getting a surprise.
In this world you don't have
To get hurt
Or hurt someone,
Just to make someone realize...
They should value your family
And every friend,
As love should be pure
Don't let it come to
An end...

Moments of POETRY

Strong times

Got to be strong

Got to make up my mind.

We can't always turn back

The hands of time,

Every day it's a struggle...

Every day we are getting in trouble.

Keep your loved ones close

And your enemies closer,

As nothing in this world happens

Like it's supposed ta....

Moments of POETRY

Someone

Got to get somewhere,
From nowhere,
Got to be someone than a 'no one'.
Going to come out sending
My messages
Full of love.
As love in life is a real need,
For those who have it
You see them happy.
They succeed and
Live it up.
If you really want to live life:
Love everybody
Not just husband and wife.
Loving the world —
That now is a part of my life....

Moments of POETRY

After Affects

Days followed by nights
I struggle to forget her.
Hope in this life of mine
Things get better.
Every day I go out facing
A new vendetta.
More than ever, it feels
Like I need you.
Too bad, as you believe you
Can now do better.
No longer want to be my friend,
Thanks for the beautiful relationship
From start to end...

Moments of POETRY

All Alone

Nasty being all alone

Not a second you feel good.

As you can't stop looking at your phone

Only to realize that she has not called

I'm still sitting alone...

Lonely days without you girl

Along with lonely nights.

Without you girl,

Everything feels so wrong and nothing

Feels right!

Moments of POETRY

Reminiscing

Every day she gives me
So many reasons to smile,
Hope she never forgets me.
Hope my number is the first
She dials
Every time she picks up her phone.
Understand that as long as I'm breathing
You're never alone.
Since you are gone
I have been told you can hear
A little emotion
In my tone...
I wake up every day
To think of you first
Thing in the morning,
Even way before I yawn....
I get upset and annoyed when I don't
See your missed calls on my phone...
Only to realize now we are alone.
Hope you're OK
As we haven't spoken in days
I want you to know
I will love you always...

Moments of POETRY

Advisory...

Nice to see you stay committed
To every commitment
Apart from this one
Because when I needed you most
You were gone.
I can't believe you haven't contacted
Me in three days
How do you get so strong?
Where did we go wrong!
Don't know anything at all
I promise you as long as I'm around
I won't let you fall
Now pick up your phone and call...

Moments of POETRY

Crazy Love

I now stand as your crazy lover

After you baby

There is no other.

I understand you

Have to walk away

For the sake of your mother and the situation

Isn't the best

But I want you to know that

I'm always here to comfort you

When you need to get away

From the stress

The effect you have my angel

Is different from the rest

For me girl, you were

The best

Moments of POETRY

Memory Lane

Sitting here in my memory lane
Without you baby.
There will be a lot of suffering, a lot of pain
Without you I can't be the same.
All I do is recite your name
Day and night
What I feel for you is too right
Who do I battle with?
Who do I fight?
Since you walked away
I don't feel right...

Moments of POETRY

Touch

Damn, I miss your touch
I miss you too much.
I want to call; want to talk;
Want to know if you're OK.
Want to find a way
For you to stay
In my life.
Always love me like a lover
Love me like a friend.
If the love we share is true
Don't walk away.
As I need you girlfriend
Representing Thre3dee.
Your love is what made me,
Every day you were there
To amaze me...

Moments of POETRY

Moments

Moments together and days

Apart.

Without you baby

It feels like I'm

Tormenting my heart.

I wish I could go back to the start

Never would I let it come to an end.

I just want to say forever

I want to love you girlfriend...

Moments of POETRY

No explanation

I can no longer explain

My pain.

I'm lost for words,

As it's hard to remain the same.

Don't know how you are

Still look back and imagine you in my car.

Cherishing every memory

Even the sweet rice.

Our combination is like fire and ice

You may not like it

But only together we look

Nice

Moments of POETRY

Open invite

They say distance makes

The heart grow.

But how do I check up on my love

And know

If she is ok.

As I can't bother her

What she believes is right.

I just want her to know that she is not

Alone. This is our fight.

Let's push away our differences

As these arms shout out

For you

With an open invite.

Moments of POETRY

Break up

Over 48 hours and still
Counting
The torture and pain
Now seriously
Amounting.
Don't worry, I'm not
Counting.
You do your thing
Whilst my love is suffering.
As you say
You can't go against
Your beliefs.
So, I don't ring
I'm no king.
But forever you're my Queen
Missing you loads
Over two years
Since you were
Last seen

Moments of POETRY

Why?

Don't know why between us
You bring the distance.
You always walk away from
My love and friendship
In the 1st instance you get
All the love we share.
How can you forget?
I was the one you said that
Thought you how to love,
Now my love wants to be gone.
Just want to let you know
That I'm not coming
Back
Until I actually become someone.
As for me baby
You're the one.

Moments of POETRY

Welcome Back!

She is back in my life like the
Morning sun
Bright and shine, hope till the end
Of time
You remain mine
As girl there isn't any other word
To describe you but as
Mine.
Your smile, your love and everything
About you
Does miracles girl
You're a lot more than just fine
Want to give you every part of me,
My heart and beat.
You're the one promise
On whom
I would never cheat.
I still remember seeing you
The last time
I dropped you off
At the bottom of your street!

Moments of POETRY

Mission love

Don't know if I should call her
Or send her a text.
As when she can't hide her love
She gets vexed.
I want you to be a part
Of my style,
The secret behind my smile.
Want to love you forever not just
A little while.
You're the one I'm missing,
Always want to be kissing.
Getting you back one day
Is another mission.

Moments of POETRY

Miss Right

Girl, you're like my paradise
On earth
My love doesn't come easy
But you're definitely worth it.
Give me another chance;
Let's work at it.
It's not the same boo
You were so loving and so true.
I swear I can't sleep at night.
All I know is that, without
You girl this isn't right.
With you I can never argue
And never fight.
Because right from the start
Baby my heart told my mind
That this is definitely
Miss right...

Moments of POETRY

Hurting

Calling this another hurt day.
As she is not with me
And it's her birthday.
I wish I could be there
With her to make things better
As I know you are going to leave me girl.
How will I ever do better?
Nine days before your birthday
You left me.
We haven't spoken.
I still miss and love you
Take it as
An appreciation token.

Moments of POETRY

Without a doubt

I had one wish and I wished for you
Not like all wishes did my wish
Come true.
Now, I sit here treasuring
Every moment I shared with you.
Yet only moments apart
And only days away
I am just sitting here trying to pray
Hoping you are doing good and fine.
I miss those days when you were mine.
I can't believe it girl
Love everything about you
Never did I doubt you
Now I need you back
Like a life line.

Moments of POETRY

That day

Can't believe how I got so lonely
As I want to love
My one and only girl
I can't believe,
I can't even think without you?
I'll be fine
Everything else in this world
May be material
But I know you are mine.
The only thing different about us
Is probably a star sign
And the year of birth
But I know you were put
For me on earth
To take all my love
You're my one Inspiration
That makes me smile.
Want to walk through the universe
Starting from this very instance
I gave my heart to you over the phone
When we both sat at a distance

Moments of POETRY

Special one

Her love was so special

Yet so true.

In this world, I feel lost

Walking around like someone who no longer

have a clue?

All my life

I can be happier if

I was next to you.

I know you're not a diamond

Or a pearl

But to me girl

You mean my whole world.

I can be yours and

You can be mine

Even though we are

Running out of time

Just understand

How much

I want you to be mine.

Moments of POETRY

Struggling

Life gets so hard.
How can everything become an outrage?
You may work 9 -5
Or 4 -12,
When you don't spend time
With your family
You are told to blame yourself
As every day is a struggle.
You can go looking for help
You may come across trouble.
Too bad, no one can put themselves
In your shoes.
How you make ends meet;
It's so hard you leave
No clues.
Everybody
I want to change the world
Forgetting the Stone Age
How is it possible?
If every living cost go up
Apart from minimum wage!

Moments of POETRY

Another light

Showing you things from
Another light,
My lyrics straight from the heart.
Want you to hold on tight
It may show you how to love
Your loved ones.
Like the way a moon show up at night.
Keep going for the moon.
Not the sky as the moon
Is the one higher than the sky?
Just above the star.
No matter whom you are
I'm sure you can relate.
It's not always easy to get money
To serve yourself a hot plate.
The Lord created one world
Keep loving don't relate with hate.
As he who is a stranger
Today we may refer to
Tomorrow
As my mate.

Moments of POETRY

Happy birthday

Just want to wish you on this special day
Happy birthday.
Hope you're happy, not feeling alone.
If you do, you can call my phone,
Can't let you be on your own.
As loneliness is a curse
By being on your own you are only
Going to get worse.
Wanted to see you again and again,
Can't believe you no longer want to be
My lover or girlfriend.
This isn't the way things should end.
Miss everything about you like your special touch.
In this life of mine, I appreciate you very much.
Come back here girl,
I miss your touch.
It's so hard that in ages
I haven't heard your voice
Walking away from you is painful.
It's not by choice.
Miss you every day love and respect you
Forever
Happy; I pray girl you stay
Forever.

Moments of POETRY

On earth

On earth I need you
Baby.
Just like the world needs
Its daylight.
Without you I'm
Self-destructing.
On my inside
In everyday having a new fight
If I let you go away
What else do I have in my life?
Who will motivate me every day?
Comfort me every night
Without you how can I be?
Right?

Moments of POETRY

Where have you been?

Lately, it's bad as we don't get to talk
I wish we could be somewhere
With just me and you
Baby, your love is so special; so true,
I'm glad the Lord made me for you.
As In this life I always need you.
As my motivation,
I can't wait to be back in your arms.
Girl, it's an amazing situation.
I can't believe.
I wait for you every night,
Even though, I know you're asleep.
Hope you remain mine
Forever girl.
As you're the one I want
To keep...

Moments of POETRY

I want to

Never went to Harlem
Or Oxford.
Moving forward on my own accord
Surname being Alam,
Love of my life never
Thought it could be my reality.
It's hard to understand
Why you couldn't commit.
Too bad every time
I was trying to be yours.
You gave me a problem
To all the cures
I'm never going to hate you...
No matter how bad
You want me to....
I'm going to love you
The way I do
Because that's what
I was made to do.

Moments of POETRY

Your wish

You wanted to break away
Me from you
Your wish was granted now it's true.
No longer, do you think
Together we could be
As it all started getting hard
Like a little bird.
You wanted to be set free
Now baby I sit lonely.
As you're without me
Hope you still
Give me a thought.
You probably
Now understand
What we had
Couldn't be bought

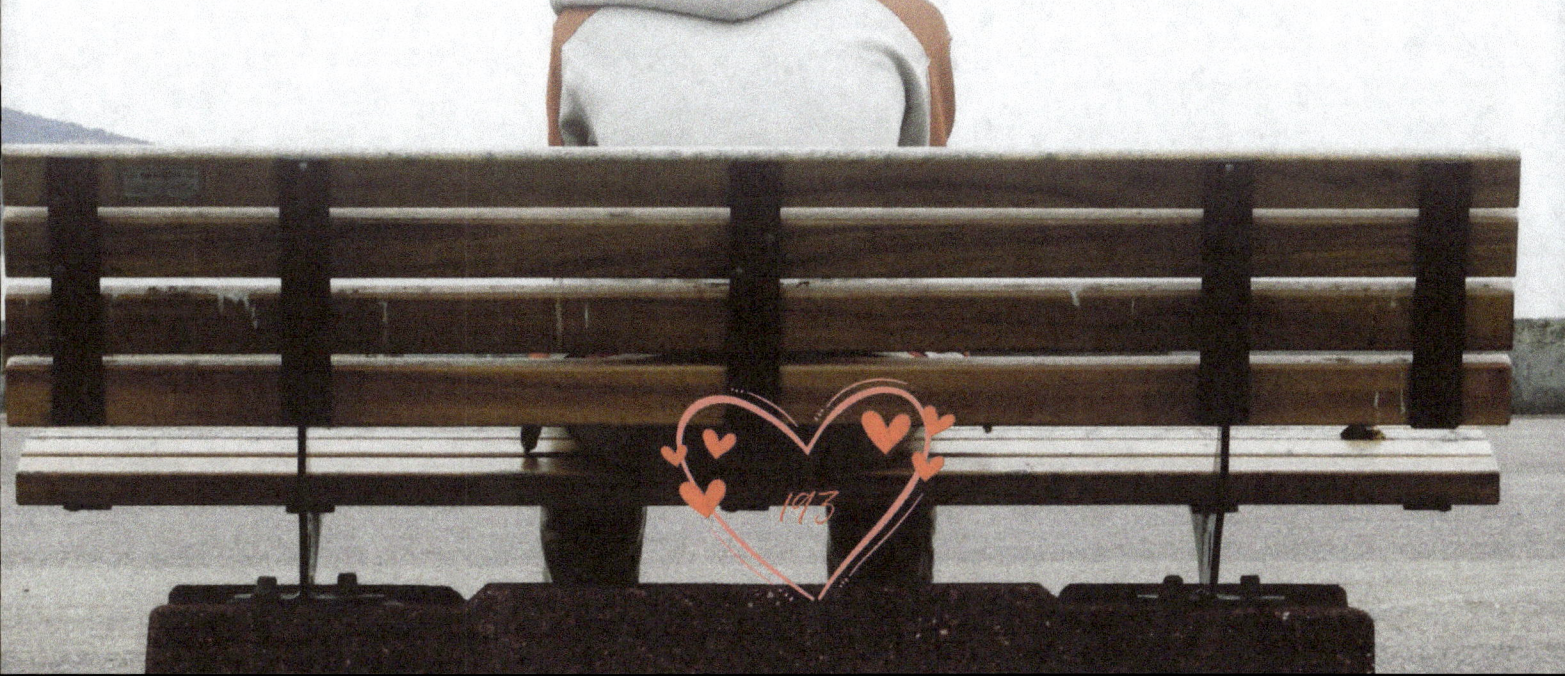

Moments of POETRY

Legendary Mum

This is just a story about the legend
Known as mum
It's so amazing the way
You made every house
A home
Never let your family alone
When they cried to you
All over the telephone
Telling you about their problems
You always go out of your way
Mamma to make the
Wrong back to right
You are my Inspiration
Mamma, without you my life
Would be just misery
And drama.
With loads of pain
The Lord put us together.
Like a Heart and a brain
Mamma I know you always
Got my back.
Your love is right you never

Moments of POETRY

Let your kids off track.
There were five of us
And you are the one
That we all love and respect
Loving you mum
For us you are
Everything!
Sorry for all the Suffering.

Moments of POETRY

Walk Away

You want to forget about us
Being together.
Walk away,
I sit in a deep conversation
With the Lord
Asking to show me a way
Which is right and I can
Make you stay.
You're the one
I love in every day.
You were around me
And my struggle everyday
In every way.
Just want to say you're the one I
Love.
Relationship pure as pain
Your name is the only one
In my heart and brain.
Don't let it all finish
And come to an end.
If I can't be your lover
You still got me as a friend.
Hope the love and understanding
We share
Never comes to an end.

Moments of POETRY

Happy 21st

Want to be the first to wish you
Happy birthday as today
You become 21.
Hope you achieve all the
Happiness that life has to offer to one.
Keep smiling; no matter
What happens, don't change
The way you are.
You are very special love...
Happy birthday I'm sure you are
My blessing from above...

Moments of POETRY

I wonder

Was it love or a phase?
Are these lonely
Days and nights temporary
Or without you
Forever they will remain.
We both knew it was
Coming to an end
But it really killed me
When you said
I can no longer
Be your friend.

Moments of POETRY

Special Bond

We haven't been together for
Too long.
It's amazing girl —
How we are together
Holding a special bond
Will never do you wrong
You're the one
I keep going on about in every song.
You doubted me
Never thought we could get married.
You are the one my life
Wanted around forever
Even if all you ever
Wanted was to be carried.
You call me your one in a million
I call you my lucky charm.
Need you here close to my heart
Away from any harm.
Every day
I ring just to say I love you baby
Can never walk away
As you're my one here I want
You to stay.

Moments of POETRY

Sacrifice

Didn't treat you bad and I didn't cheat
Too bad when we separated.
You said no longer
Can we speak?
Or meet.
I asked why?
You said it's against all you believe
As you don't want to lose anyone you love.
So, you are going to sacrifice your lover
It's hard not to text or ring.
Your name is all I am reciting
Want to call you
And tell you, you're my all
But I understand
You're no longer here to watch me
Rise and fall
Still when the pain gets too much
Your name is what I call.
The Lord is the one with mercy.
We all remain in need of guidance
As we are thirsty
For love and peace
Trouble is at its peak.
Let's bring back unity
For everybody not just you and me

Moments of POETRY

Falling Apart

Falling apart without you
I once was the guy who inspired
People with a clean heart and mind
After being in love now,
I sit here with a shattered
Heart along with a broken mind,
Up till four in the morning
Missing you so bad baby.
So restless but still I'm not yawning
Over a month.
Since I last heard your voice
And still you're not ringing.
Girl! separation was your choice
Without you I don't feel like getting out of
Isolation
Never mind making noise in the current
Situation

Moments of POETRY

Our time

Need to get a bite to eat
Even though it's you I meet
I can tell by your body language baby.
You want me to sweep you off your feet
It's not Halloween but tonight.
You may just get a trick or treat
Me and you girl were put together
Like the hands of time.
Every hour you make my coocoo
Celebrate as you
Return back to being mine.
Happy to see you my lady
Without you 59 minutes
Drives me crazy.
Then on the hour you amaze me
You got me on the move every minute
Whilst for me you move on the hour
Blossom baby blossom
You're my flower

Moments of POETRY

Humanity

Humanity has been saying all along
When are we all going to come
Together to stay strong?
Can't get rid of any one
The Lord put us together to stay strong.
Guide each other if we ever get lost together
We shall find the way
Unity will help us
To stop going wrong…

Moments of POETRY

Still Missing

Every Friday like before
On your street
I want to take a drive.
The truth is soul mate without you
It only gets hard to
Survive.
Need you back here
I know back then I called you wifey
And my girl.
But after I lost you
I now understand
I lost my world.
You're the perfect gift
From destiny.
Girl,
If it wasn't for you
I couldn't have find
Love within me.

Moments of POETRY

You only

It's becoming sad and lonely
I want and need you only.
After you there isn't
Going to be another.
I rather stay lonely.
I sit and analyze every memory
Feeling traumatized.
Can't believe you're
No longer with me
All you left me with
Were tears in
My eyes

Moments of POETRY

Mr. or Mrs. Right

You say you need and want someone
To treat you good.
He needs to be good looking
And really strong.
He doesn't have to be good at heart
But like you he has to be
Academically bright
He doesn't have to love me
Just keep tugging me Mr. Right.
You're looking for your wifey
When it's only skirts and heels.
You don't want her to be materialistic
But that's all I can feel.
You want to change her
From miss independent
To miss housewife.
You really want to torture
And torment her,
Is this your definition?
Of miss right?

Moments of POETRY

Destruction

Lady, women, girl
Need you to understand
That without you
I feel nothing but destruction.
In my world
Lady, women, girl,
Every day I thank the Lord
For sending you to me.
Without you, no longer can I be.
Chilling with the one I love…
All day and night…
Cuddles and kisses throughout
The day…
Pillow fights at night…
Since I lost you girl there isn't
No other name I could ever recite…
Our love was supposed
To touch a new height
I called you wifey whilst you called
Me Mr. Right
Funny, how it all came to an end
Can't forget that night….

Moments of POETRY

I see Love

Days going by and I don't get
To hear your voice.
Understand baby,
This is your doing
Not my choice.
Every day I search for you
Even though I never find you
Thanking the Lord for blessing
Me with eyes,
As they say love is blind.
You feel me,
You didn't have to
Be a murderer
You didn't need
To kill
The growing chemistry!

Moments of POETRY

Misunderstood

Many have struggled
Some have been
Loved and cuddled.
What about that one man
That's in such a muddle?
All this time what
I thought was mine
Simply wasn't.
Everything I understood
No longer stands.
Felt really hurt
When you let go of my
Hand.

Moments of POETRY

Exam time

Exam time —
You're focusing on revision
Too bad girl we are
Living in a division
I know, it's a hard time
As you are always
Getting stressed
You have been giving the books
A lot of our time
I'm here to support you.
Making you strong, my texts
Show up like motivation.
Never going to do you wrong?
I don't want to go to war
I'm not a soldier.
Just want to let you know I'll be there
Every time the world gets colder.
When you really need a shoulder
Don't want to sit there saying Damn!
Should have told you girl
I'm upset as I never got to hold ya!
Your smile is a real savior.
It has a big impact on my behavior.

Moments of POETRY

Express yourself

Stop your denying

Notice me trying

For the sake of those special memories.

Please stop crying

No longer can I see you burn.

Every day

It seems to be getting worse.

Why am I getting screwed?

Who was the one to send down the curse?

Every day I feel like I'm losing

My piece of mind.

Where do I have to search

For me to find?

Cheer up cheer up

You're like a beautiful sky

I'm waiting for you to clear up

Do whatever but don't

Stress yourself

Come express yourself.

Moments of POETRY

Sky is the limit

Shakespeare said it's better to have
Loved and lost than not love at all.
Do what you got to do baby
I'll await your call
My Miss 07850.
Today, make it a yes as
No longer can I cope with a no…
Missing you more everyday
Why can't I get you back here?
Forever I want you to stay.
The sky is the limit
They are not letting me to my feet;
I struggle every day.
As I have demons trying to snatch what
I'm trying to eat
Please God help me slow down
My heartbeat
Feels like I'm
Being a beat down
On repeat!

Moments of POETRY

Crazy times

Preach; preach life a lesson for me here
To help & teach
We have come to a time
Where babies are having babies.
What used to be good now just seems
Crazy — everybody
Going through a phase
Or is it just being lazy...
You need to give it to get it
And it's important
You need to get it to give it
No matter what.
We are not
The same if we forget it.
Respect

Moments of POETRY

Busy world

We all are part of a busy world
Where no one can spare
A bit of time.
Everybody is fighting over
What's yours and mine.
Bad boys need to stop treating
Good girls bad.
Good girls need to stop thinking
A loser who is here.
To use you
Can't be the best you've ever had.

Moments of POETRY

Miracles

Need you in my life
More than ever.
Girl, in my life you're the first
Miracle
I call a treasure.
Everything is amazing
Even though we aren't
Sleeping together.
It's beautiful how we trust each other
Even with our eyes closed.
Real love doesn't just turn up
If you take off your clothes
Every man is really just after
One thing.
It all depends on you baby
What you are offering.
Her friends said like all men
I was only after one thing.
Too bad after hearing that crap you end
Up leaving.
Was it really worth believing?
As we both lost out

Moments of POETRY

Someone that meant the most
I used to wait
For you as if you were a letter.
As I awaited the post
Thought of you every morning
Where shall I deliver my post?

Moments of POETRY

No Matrix

I admit that I could never make
A matrix
But to keep you safe
In a happy
Home
I'll do anything; even
Handpick the bricks.
No magic so no rabbit
Out the hat tricks.
You're not temporary as a
Baby; you're a permanent fix.
I'll sooth you
Let me know if you want to inhale.
I'll be your Vicks.
Girl you're special
I call you a blessing.
Every time you are around me
Baby it stops me from stressing.
We could just talk, we don't have to
Be kissing and caressing
Forever I'm yours.
Don't ever think I
Could be missing.

Moments of POETRY

My Love

You want my love
Along with all my attention.
How I feel nobody cares
As no one wants me to mention.
For you baby I made change after change
Just so that
I don't fit in now
As I feel all strange.
Clean heart with clean intention
I love you more
Without any hesitation
Too bad it hurts
Because of your inconsistency.
In this big world I feel all alone
because of you girl — every two seconds
I'm looking at my phone
Knowing you're not going to call.
I ain't get my heart up as it constantly
Wants to fall.
Too bad girl, you weren't willing to work
On our issues.
Can't believe Kleenex is more reliable
When it's only tissues.

Moments of POETRY

Law

Fell in love with a law student, who at the start
Said we shouldn't and couldn't
But we got past that.
Too bad;
Your love for me
Was overruled
I walked away feeling plunked out
And fooled
I was trying to support her
With my love as she
Had exams;
Didn't even know
That she no longer gives a damn
About me
Keep listening to your friends
Pushing happiness
Away
I'm going to turn my dreams into
Reality
When I achieve it
I'll come back your way.

Moments of POETRY

Interaction

There was a time that we could all
Communicate and interact,
Even if you were walking
alone.
Even when I compliment
You don't know
As you listen to your headphones.
She had the word, 'flirt' written
On her neck chain
I said it's OK baby if you have been hurt.
I want to exchange
Your number for my name.
I'm going to erase all your pain
All you're ever
Going to remember
Is my name
She said need you all
Over me
It's a lot deeper than any fantasy
Girl, you are addictive,
Shall I
Call you ecstasy!

Moments of POETRY

My Mistake

I'm sorry for loving you girl;
Call it my mistake.
I have done everything for you
Never thought of what I can take.
Too bad you were inconsistent —
Showing me that you're a snake
I even worked at Burger King
Selling them king fries.
I may not be a king
But my queen I need you
To realize that
I'm nothing like the other guys.
Do you really hate me for the way
I am and was?
Wanted to make the
World a better place
Where happiness
Can go onto every face,
Forgetting color and race.
If one man can change the world
I want to be the one.
Hope I get my chance
Before from this world
I'm gone

Moments of POETRY

Never did I cheat on you girl
So, I can't be guilty.
Don't know why
You left me but without you
I feel filthy.

Moments of POETRY

Midnight Crush

I have seen things you've never seen.
That's why on you girl
I've always been keen.
Wanted to make you reality
Too bad you wanted to leave me
Like a dream.
Still remember our first kiss
Made me feel
Good and lush.
Without you
I move on a rush.
Still baby I need you to know —
You're my midnight crush.

Moments of POETRY

Self-explanatory

One day will you come back
To explain your actions
As you tortured my brain?
As I had no clue
Why I lost my love?
Why boo?
Where did we go wrong?
I'm going to make it for us
As my love is true
Baby all I want to say is
I'm nothing without you.

Moments of POETRY

A thought

A thought within a thought:
Why does it feel like
I'm the only one who knows?
With money and material,
Happiness can't be bought.
Love is supposed to be blind,
Humans are supposed to be kind
Instead you can forever search.
But you may still not find
As everyone is searching for something
Rather than someone
Too bad even quicker than
Me meeting you
You were gone...
If diamonds are a girl's best friend
I can't be just a stone.
If happiness is about being together
No longer can I
Be alone.
I can't forget those nights
When all night we would be
On the phone

Moments of POETRY

From being the perfect soul mate

You went to being a stranger.

Forever for you my love was pure

Why you look at it as danger

You stopped keeping in touch

All I now do is miss you very much.

Moments of POETRY

The past

I can't believe everything we shared
Is now in the past
Too bad the love we once shared
Wasn't meant to last
I figured you're not happy
With your figure
You should always be the same person
You are on the inside.
No matter if on the outside you get
Smaller or bigger
When the going gets tough the
Tough gets going
I love you girl is the fact that
You should know.
Every day you increase the distance
You dispose me like I'm
Just a material substance
First, I see you on the street
Couldn't help but to put
My heart at your feet
It's not Halloween
But I'll invent you a trick
Before I take you out for a treat

Moments of POETRY

The other days,
I was thinking about all the
Times in the past
When I was yours and you were mine
Wishing we could go back
With the hands of time

Moments of POETRY

Deactivating

Keep running girl, deactivating
Every account.
My love will haunt you;s
Forever it's on
A serious amount.
Pretty woman no longer do we
Need to fantasize.
As every dream you wanted
To make reality
Is here before your eyes.
You're going to run away or realize
I'm here to love you not fantasize.
I've seen you doing pedicure
And manicure on others
But you're the
One I adore.
Looking amazing and blessed
With that perfect smile,
I could never be
Stressed.

Moments of POETRY

Marriage

You're the one
I can't lose
As you're the one
My heart had to choose.
Smile so perfect; look and feel
Like a rose.
How do I stop myself from proposing?
Never would I abuse
Or use you — I'm not a clock.
So, don't try to snooze
As I'm all you really got and
You don't want to lose.
Marriage is supposed to be
Pure as water
It's not just about making
Your family happy
Unhappily bringing
Home someone else's
Son or daughter!

Moments of POETRY

Missing

I miss you and
I know you miss me too.
I love you but girl
No idea if you do too.
Everything we had was
Amazing and true
I just wish we could go back to
Me and you.
It's funny how a bad decision
Brought us to an end
I stand around town
Looking at so many faces
Want to cut the chases.
Been a long time
Since you were last seen
Even though your face re-appears
In my dreams,
When I wake up to
You not being there,
I scream.
I'm stressed but not
Going to blame it on
Alopecia
It's just me having to
Live without you.
When it's really bad,
I need you.

Moments of POETRY

Get Together

No more girl can I live
Like this day and night.
Come back girl
Let's make whatever
Was wrong right.
You didn't stop
Loving me so
Why should I.
Without you
I feel weak
I don't know how to
Stop myself from
Crying
Without you
I lost everything.
My heart and mind
Keep telling me
I'm dying
I seek shelter
In the rain.
For you, I carry
Unconditional love
Whilst you carry
Unconditional pain,

Moments of POETRY

Too bad you don't feel the same.
We are on time
You're a lot more
Than just fine
Can't resist the temptation
Think this summer
I need to make you mine.

Moments of POETRY

Vision

All I remember was you doing
Your revision
Not showing me your vision.
As no longer did you and me want
To stand.
I can't believe you just
Let go of my hand...
You said you love me
I'm guessing you never knew
What it meant.
I was financially broke that time
But in your love
I've overspent.
Now where do I find
A real lover and repent
You changed to be hard and heartless
Like cement.
Sitting here every day watching
The sunshine too bad
I still can't figure out girl
Why you are not mine
You told me you never wanted me

Moments of POETRY

Lying or crying,
When in reality you left me in a state
Where you can easily see I was
Dying
Never once did you look back
As everybody
Set me as a target.
Now
I feel like I'm under attack.

Moments of POETRY

Next time

I love you girl wishing you all the happiness
You just need to find the strength
The next time you tell someone
You love them
Make sure it's truly meant.
That was another day and now this is another.
The way in which you left me don't
Think I can move on to another.
You chose to mess with my head
You know I wasn't after one thing
I never rushed you to bed instead my love
Was true
You say anything girl
I will make sure
I make it true for you
No longer do you feel the need
To see me or my happiness
I sit all alone missing your texts
Hearing your voice on the phone

Moments of POETRY

Cross path

Can't believe we walked
Past each other
In the opposite path:
The feeling after seeing your pretty face
This is going to last
For a long while
There isn't any denial
No matter how close I come
You push me away.
Why don't you understand?
Girl, the Lord put me here as an answer to
Your prayers.
This man swears as though you're the one
For whom I truly want and care,
For you I will always rise.
You're more precious than any surprise
Come back and realize
My baby I'm not typical like every other guy.
On you baby
I would never cheat or lie.
Seeing you girl, after so long

Moments of POETRY

Don't know how we just walked past each other.

Felt like it was so wrong

Couldn't show you my emotions

As I need you to be strong.

Felt like my fresh wounds

Were being picked.

Trouble in the pain felt

Like my nuts were kicked

Moments of POETRY

Loving Mum

I'm no genie so can't grant your wishes
I'll do anything for you, even your dishes.
Mum I love you forever,
Need you to understand.
You're my world mum.
You're my treasure —
Can never let go of your hand.
You're the greatest Mother and
I need you to understand
I can't replace you with any other.
Your love is unconditional.
I've found you very
Inspirational
And educational but
I worry about you daily.
You seem to have been getting
Vulnerable. You're my one
Lady I can never stand to see in
Trouble

Moments of POETRY

Fake relations

Now let's look at all our fake relations—
People with
No character, morals or patience.
They are different in the morning,
and at night.
Why shall we believe?
When all they do is
Come back to deceive.
If you need someone to talk to
These faking relations shout
Whenever you need a hand
They are never about.
Got my own kids along
With nephews and nieces
No more are these fake relations
Going to rip my family
To pieces.

Moments of POETRY

Apologies

We were both a part of each other's
Life
You were my everything;
I even wanted
To make you my wife.
When you left me,
I felt like you slit my throat.
Remember you used to tell me
You love me
For what I wrote.
I am not perfect.
I accept even when I've done wrong,
Want to apologize to everyone.
I hope you understand!
I'm sorry
Isn't just a word
I'm sorry!
Forget the past as
We have all done wrong.
Unite today
Let's get along

Moments of POETRY

Criticism

Families are quick to criticize.
When will we realize,
To stop doing each other over
As we're upsetting
That lady we both call mother.
My religion teaches peace
And unity
Peace is for everyone
Not just you and me.
All my life I had to go
In search of the truth
Never was understood until
I found the real me in the booth.
Love everyone the old and the youth
Knowledge is power and that's the truth.
You never loved me
That's why you lose me.
Forever I want you
But that's seriously going to cost me.
Can't call my vision
Strange as the world
Is awakening my hopes

Moments of POETRY

And my dreams are
Now commonly seen.
Every week the lotto's hitting
Jackpots
Sometimes, a rollover is
So much money going
Around and still we live in recession
With very little progression.

Moments of POETRY

You let Down

I'm sorry for you letting
Me down.
Don't worry, I'm still in town.
Religion, love, unity and peace
I got to search until I find.
Got to get this poverty
Off my mind.
Preach! preach this is our turn.
Take it all in;
We got loads to
Teach.
We've all got loads to learn
Respect, honor and dignity
Is here.
Give it to get it.
Your mother
Raised you good.
Don't you ever
Forget it.
Increase the peace
Always be loving & kind
If you really want answers
You need
To search and find.

Moments of POETRY

Kids

The Lord blessed me
With a
Son and a Daughter
Any day I'll rise to
Support them
As they are innocent and very
Special.
When a day goes by
When I haven't
See them
I feel troubled.
Hope I can raise them to
My best.
My kids are so amazing
As I'm happy in them.
It is time
I get to invest.
Never want the three
Of you
To feel neglected.
The Lord put me here
To make sure

Moments of POETRY

You guys are protected —
Never want you to feel
Lonely or sad.
As everyone loves you
But you also got a
Very loving
Dad!

Moments of POETRY

Without you

Confession time.
Girl, I can't stand the silence.
It's killing and hurting me
Like violence,
Feeling like a guitar
Without a string.
How will I be able
To remain myself
Living up to the whole thing...
Every day you say it's our time
But you never get there.
Girl it's like you're
Lying,
Without you
Every day I see myself
Dying
You're pushing me away every day
How do I get my heart and mind
To stay strong?
Without you girl, I'm going wrong.
Need to make it right.
I'm the dude you used to kiss good night
Without you girl,
I gasp like an eye for a tear
Like a crowd for a cheer.
With all being said
I need you back here!!

Moments of POETRY

Live once

We all say that you only live once...
But then you got life after death...
I pray to My Lord that I'm positive
till my last breath.
Remain true and never would I lie.
Stop abusing yourselves as you don't
need to cry...
never would I turn my back on you
never would we have to deny...
I rather give you my honesty
as nowadays
It's become easy to lie...

Moments of POETRY

I Care

Every day we look for love
When you should be
Looking for a lover.
It's funny how some people
Move around
From one, and then
To another.
It's disastrous how a young school girl
Can become a mother...
It is real, people
From part of our nation
Stop sleeping around
I'm not here to promote contraception.
But I know they sell it for a pound.

Moments of POETRY

Pain

Got loads running through my mind,
Pain got me lost
In translation
Why am I still searching
When I struggle to find?
Got no one around me but pain
I didn't participate.
But still got entered into this game
Where I'm losing more than what
I'm winning
They didn't tell me it would
Be like this from the beginning
Like others I can't believe
We voted for our own destruction
This model doesn't support
Reproduction

Moments of POETRY

Rightright

This feeling is
So right.
I want to hold you in my arms.
Close to my chest.
Love you forever
Love you to my best
I want you only so stop
Talking about the rest.
I had to come close, had to confess
Without you baby.
All I ever do is stress.
I'm being honest and won't
Ever do you wrong.
I'm crying my heart out,
Won't ever give you a reason
To be upset
Or be lonely as you are all mine
And mine only.
Now you got me feeling so, so right
Want to keep you with me
At all time; no need to lie
After I met you girl
I really am a
Changed guy!

Moments of POETRY

Roses Are Red....

Roses are red

Violets are blue

What am I supposed to do?

In this world without you

A feeling even better than

Sexual healing

Can't hide my inner feeling.

That's why now

I'm revealing

That you're the one

My heart

Can't stop feeling for.

Please never walk away

From my side

What you receive

From others may look like love.

Whilst they want to take you

On a ride

What's the point of loving you?

If my feelings are supposed to be hidden

Got to confess

I want to love to my best.

As from this

Moment onwards it is me and you

Living blessed.